Praise for *Practical Candle Magic*

"I have been practicing magic for over fifty years, and all the things my grandma ever taught me about candle magic are in *Practical Candle Magic*, and much more. This is a veritable encyclopedia on the topic that spans many cultures and is a must-have for any witch, beginner to advanced. The reader will find spells, exercises, mantic divinations, a compendium of correspondences, how to divine with pins in candles, wax poppets, and much more. This book is a valuable resource. Rachel Patterson writes in an easy style that is relevant to our more modern times. *Practical Candle Magic* will not disappoint and is sure to be a bestseller!"

—Cat Gina Cole, author of *Psychic Skills for Magic & Witchcraft*

"Rachel Patterson has brought candle magic to life in exciting new ways with this book. Filled with practical information and techniques, examples to use and personalize, details on how to dispose of magical ingredients, tips for cleansing and re-using—there is so much crammed into this delightful book. *Practical Candle Magic* offers new takes on candle magic for the novice or those with experience, and it will be a valuable resource to rely on for years to come. Written in a warm and welcoming manner with a depth of knowledge and insight founded in real experience, this book deserves a place on every Pagan bookshelf."

—Moira Hodgkinson, author of
Operation Cone of Power and *Living Witchcraft*

T0049965

PRACTICAL
CANDLE
MAGIC

About the Author

Rachel Patterson, also known as the "Kitchen Witch," is a High Priestess of the Kitchen Witch Coven and an Elder at the online Kitchen Witch School of Witchcraft. She's the author of twenty-five books on Witchcraft, including *Curative Magic* and *A Witch for Every Season*. She is a regular contributor to *Pagan Dawn* magazine and *Fate and Fortune* magazine and speaks at Pagan events. Rachel was added to Watkins' Spiritual 100 List for 2023. She lives in Hampshire, England. Visit her at www.RachelPatterson.co.uk.

PRACTICAL
CANDLE
MAGIC

Witchcraft with Wick & Wax

RACHEL PATTERSON

Llewellyn Publications | Woodbury, Minnesota

FIRST EDITION
First Printing, 2023

Book design by Samantha Peterson
Cover design by Kevin R. Brown
Interior art by Llewellyn Art Department

Photography is used for illustrative purposes only. The persons depicted may not endorse or represent the book's subject.

Llewellyn Publications is a registered trademark of Llewellyn Worldwide Ltd.

Library of Congress Cataloging-in-Publication Data (Pending)
ISBN: 978-0-7387-7153-3

Llewellyn Worldwide Ltd. does not participate in, endorse, or have any authority or responsibility concerning private business transactions between our authors and the public.

All mail addressed to the author is forwarded but the publisher cannot, unless specifically instructed by the author, give out an address or phone number.

Any internet references contained in this work are current at publication time, but the publisher cannot guarantee that a specific location will continue to be maintained. Please refer to the publisher's website for links to authors' websites and other sources.

Llewellyn Publications
A Division of Llewellyn Worldwide Ltd.
2143 Wooddale Drive
Woodbury, MN 55125-2989
www.llewellyn.com

Printed in the United States of America

Other Books by Rachel Patterson

Disclaimer

If you have ailments or mental health issues, get them diagnosed by a medical professional. If it is advised, work out a course of medication. This book does not in any way replace the need for proper medical treatment, including medication or therapy for mental health issues. Neither the author nor the publisher advocate for self-diagnosis. Always seek professional advice.

In the following pages you will find recommendations for the use of certain herbs, essential oils, incense blends, and ritual items. If you are allergic to any of these items, please refrain from use. Each body reacts differently to herbs, essential oils, and other items, so results may vary person to person.

Essential oils are potent; use care when handling them. Always dilute essential oils before placing them on your skin, and make sure to do a patch test on your skin before use. Perform your own research before using an essential oil.

Never self-medicate, even with herbal remedies. Herbal remedies can be extremely potent; some are toxic. Others can react with prescription or over-the-counter medications in adverse ways. Please do not ingest any herbs if you aren't sure you have identified them correctly. If you are on medication or have health issues, please do not ingest any herbs without first consulting a qualified practitioner.

Contents

Part Two

Amplifying Your Magic

Part Three

Candle Magic Spells

Practices

INTRODUCTION

Lighting the Wick

I have walked the Pagan Witchcraft pathway for over thirty years now, and as a Witch, one of the first types of magic I worked with was a candle spell. Thankfully, it was also a success!

My pathway began in Wicca, gaining my three degrees and a title of High Priestess. But somewhere along the way it twisted and turned, and I have ended up in the role of Kitchen Witch, with a bit of Hedge Witch thrown in for good measure. I love to learn and am always delving into different pathways and magical practices to add to my own. My way of working magic is that of a Kitchen Witch with a heavy sprinkling of folk magic. I like to work intuitively and with whatever items I have on hand, like candles.

Candles play a huge role in my Witchcraft, whether in the form of a spell, on my altar, for devotions and dedications, or to provide light for rituals. Candle magic is my "go-to" type of magic whenever I need to work a spell. I love how candle magic can be simple or elaborate—the choice is yours. A quick "I need a spell right now" can be as straightforward as lighting one candle, or it can be incorporated into a full-on "all the bells and whistles" ritual. Candle magic gives you the opportunity to add layers to the energy with the chosen candle colour and the addition of sigils, symbols, pins, herbs, and oils. There is something very magical about candles, from the action of lighting the wick to watching the flame dance about.

Over the years, I have tried and tested many different types and varieties of candle and ways of working with them. In this book, I present to you the ways I work with practical candle magic. I also offer you information and guidelines so you can create your own magic with candles. I encourage you to tap into your own intuition and work with magic in your own way. This book is a base to start from; read the information, use the guides as a prompt, but ultimately, work with candle magic in a way that suits you. Trust your intuition; it will not let you down.

PART ONE
THE BASICS

CHAPTER ONE

Simply Candles

One example of candle magic is blowing out the candles on a birthday cake and making a wish, but that is only an extremely basic form—candle magic is so much more.

Candle magic starts with the candle, but it relies heavily on your intent. If your will and desire are strong enough, they will transfer to the candle and help move the magic along. If you are working a spell half-heartedly, then the likelihood of it being successful is slim. As with other forms of spell work, candle magic can be as grand and flamboyant or as simple as you want to make it. It is one of the easiest types of spell work: all you need is a candle, intent, and matches—yes, it really is that simple! You can increase the power of the spell by bringing in colour magic and adding layers via herbs, crystals, and other magical ingredients.

Candles also employ the element of fire. Once you light a candle, you set the spell in motion using the power of that element. Fire is powerful and must be respected. It brings transformation in many forms, along with the power of change. Fire can be destructive, but from that destruction comes rebirth and new opportunities. After all, the flame of a candle also brings light to the dark.

When you look at a candle more closely, it brings together all four elements: the flame is fire, the wick is earth, the wax is water, and the element of air is needed to allow it to burn.

Originally, of course, candles would have been practical and used to light homes. For centuries, candles have been important to many cultures, and they are typically representative of spirituality, prayer, or magic of some kind, whether the candle is lit to celebrate or perhaps lit in memory of someone who is no longer with us. Christians see the candle as Christ and his eternal light; candles are also used to commemorate saints and to show intent to support a prayer. In Judaism, nine candles set into a Hanukkah menorah are lit over eight nights to symbolise rededication to the Temple in Jerusalem. In Hinduism, Diwali is a celebration of light that features lamps called *diyas*. In Buddhism, candles are an important part of ceremonies and festivals; one of those is Thailand's Candle Festival, which includes a candle procession and elaborate wax sculptures. Candles are said to represent the enlightenment of Buddha, amongst other things. In Islam, the candle represents the "light of God" and is used in various rituals.[1]

It is important to remember that a candle and any other items you add to your spell work are just tools—tools used by us to direct and focus our intent. Ultimately, the power of a spell is within you. If your will and intent are strong, that will translate in the energy of the magic and lead to the success of the spell working. If you go into it half-heartedly or not committed to the outcome, then the spell will likely fail. You are the magic; the candles and all the other additions are merely tools.

Most importantly, relax! Some of the information and instructions given here may sound incredibly stressful or even scary. If you trust your intuition when creating and working a spell, it will not let you down. There is no right way or wrong way to do spell work, and although spells do not always work in the way we expected, they do work. Trust in your own abilities.

Fire and Flame

The flame of a candle is a manifestation of the element of fire. It is a living, breathing energy and carries the fire elemental within. Elementals are the raw primordial energy of each element, which in turn reflect nature itself; they carry the true, basic, original energy of each element. Elementals can take on any shape, size, or form they wish to.

---

1. Encyclopaedia Iranica, s.v. "candle," accessed May 30, 2023, https://www.iranicaonline.org /articles/candle-pers.

A fire elemental can be found in the form of a small candle flame, the flames in your firepit or a ritual bonfire, or even the lava and flames spewing from a volcano. The fire elemental can charge us with energy on all kinds of levels: physical, mental, emotional, and spiritual. Being able to connect with the fire elemental helps us tune in and recognise nature around us. Any flame has the spirit of a fire elemental within.

In some Wiccan traditions and New Age spirituality, you will find a hierarchy within the elemental world, with each tier being represented by a figurehead. They are all elemental spirits that embody the spirit of fire.

- Fire is ruled by King Djinn, a warrior who controls the power of life, courage, inner strength, and transformation. Images of King Djinn usually show him as a warrior type surrounded by flames. His manner and communication are incredibly direct; he doesn't mess around, very much reflecting the energy of the flame itself.

- Above him is the Archangel Michael, believed to be the first angel created. Michael is the Archangel of fire and sun who brings justice and defence. He is often called in to bring protection and to help you achieve your goals. He can be found in several fire-related stories throughout the Bible, although it should be noted that angels were found in cultures that predate Christianity. Stories of the Archangels can be found dating back to the Bronze Age.[2] Think of Archangels as being universal to all faiths. Some Wiccan traditions call in the Archangels at the quarters when in ritual. These are referred to as "Guardians of the Watchtowers." The Archangels are called "The Watchers" because they look after, or "watch," human beings. Archangels are incredibly powerful! Although I don't personally work with Archangels, I know a lot of Witches that do.

- Each elemental is represented by a form, and the fire elementals' are called salamanders. However, this is not the small lizard creature you may be familiar with. Rather, it is a fiery serpent—although what they are called is less important than the idea that the flame is a living spirit.

---

2. Sarah Crocker, "The History of Archangels Explained," *Grunge*, September 10, 2021, https://www.grunge.com/601014/the-history-of-archangels-explained/.

Connecting with the fire elemental within the flame can burn away old, unwanted, and toxic habits because fire destroys to clear and make way for new, exciting possibilities and opportunities. Connecting with the fire elemental can also help with inner work, personal power, and healing; fire elementals can assist in all kinds of ways! Just remember that fire's power is strong and not always easy to control.

In my own practice, I don't work with any hierarchy. I focus solely on the salamander, the spirit of fire found within the flame. But I put this information here in case you are drawn to call upon King Djinn or Archangel Michael—it may work for you. These fire elementals can add to the power of your spell work; invite them to lend their energy to your spell, or place an image or picture of them on your altar.

Eternal Flame

An eternal flame is defined as a "flame, lamp or torch that burns continuously for an indefinite period. Often used to commemorate a person or event of national significance, or to serve as a reminder of commitment to a common goal."[3] Eternal flames can be found at war memorials. Ancient temples had them lit and tended by priestesses in honour of deities. The Temple of Vesta is a good example. In ancient Rome, six priestesses would tend to Vesta, goddess of the hearth. Their duties included tending the perpetual fire in the Temple of Vesta.[4]

Another site of a perpetual flame is in Kildare in Ireland. Dating back to pre-Christian times, a ritual fire dedicated to the goddess Brigid was kept alight. The eternal flame continued in honour of St. Brigid when it was taken on by Christian nuns, and was thought to be alight up to the sixteenth century. In 1993 the flame was re-lit by a group called the Brigidine Sisters and has been burning ever since.[5]

---

3. Definitions, s.v. "Eternal flame," accessed May 30, 2023, https://www.definitions.net/definition/eternal+flame.

4. The Editors of Encyclopaedia Britannica, s.v. "Vestal Virgins," *Encyclopaedia Britannica Online*, last updated April 18, 2023, https://www.britannica.com/topic/Vestal-Virgins.

5. "Lighting the Perpetual Flame of Brigid (A Brief History of the Flame)," County Kildare Community Network, January 2006, https://www.kildare.ie/community/notices/perpetual-flame.asp.

It is probably unrealistic (and definitely a fire hazard) to keep a candle flame lit indefinitely in your home. But this practice can be adapted; it works particularly well for lanterns, as they are much safer to keep alight for longer periods of time. A candle or an oil lantern can be dedicated to a deity of your choice. Light the flame for a short while every evening, or while you carry out your daily devotionals.

Respecting the Flame

When doing this work, it is important to always remember that you are working with fire. There needs a bit of respect for and attention to the flame in order to keep you, others, and your personal belongings safe.

Never leave a burning candle unattended. Trust me, I know. Here is my tale of woe: I used to work my candle magic in a ceramic dish I had specifically for that purpose. It had a central dish with a "moat" around the edge. Basically, it was a small chip 'n dip dish, but it was perfect for putting a candle in the centre and surrounding it with herbs, crystals, or other magical ingredients.

I like to keep things simple, so I started with a gold candle in the centre, which I sprinkled with dried lemon balm. Around the edge, in the "moat," I put cinnamon bark, dried beans, and popped lotus seeds.

I lit the candle and sat back to watch the flame. I never leave a lit candle unattended, although sometimes I do other things in the same room, all the while keeping an eye on it. However, on this occasion, I was drawn to sit and watch.

Thankfully I did, because once the candle had burnt down to the end and was just a flame eating up the last remnants of wax that had melted onto the base, there was a loud *crack* followed by herbs and beans flying across the altar, and the dish split in two. Flames were now taking hold of the velvet cloth underneath and quickly made a start on the varnish on the sideboard.

I blew out the flames as fast as I could, but everything was too hot to handle, so I had to run and get a pair of tongs from the kitchen to pick up the burning embers to keep the fire from spreading.

The outcome was a melted hole in the velvet cloth and a scorch mark on the sideboard—and, of course, a ceramic dish that was now in two pieces.

If I had been in another room, I dread to think what would have happened, as there were plenty of flammable items on my altar, including the altar itself and several shelves of books above it. This experience was a harsh reminder that flames should not be left alone.

It bears repeating: *Candles are a fire hazard. Treat them with respect.*

This leads me to the next piece of advice. Be careful when using herbs and oils with a candle flame, as they are all highly flammable. Also bear in mind that altar cloths or other fabrics that are near the flame may be highly flammable.

One final tip: it is always advisable to allow a new pillar candle to burn long enough for the wax to melt from the centre right to the edge on its first burning. If you do not and the candle only burns long enough to melt a small ring in the centre, the candle will never burn past that on future lightings. You end up with only the centre of the candle burning, never melting the wax around the edge.

CHAPTER TWO

Witchcraft Fundamentals

Witchcraft is a magical practice, and I like to work on the premise that you can work magic by trusting your intuition—for the most part, anyway. I also believe that Witchcraft can be tailored to work for you and adjusted for your own personal journey. There is no right or wrong way to work magic, particularly when it comes to candle magic. However, there are some guidelines that can help keep things from going off the rails or, in fact, going horribly wrong. There are no strict rules, but the suggestions I have included here are worth bearing in mind and using your own judgement on. There is also no shortcut to experience; the only way to learn to work with magic is to *actually* work with it.

Ethics and Responsibility

You may already be aware, but I think it only wise to reiterate: If you work any kind of magic, then it comes with responsibility. Not just responsibility for others, but also for yourself. You are working with energy and power; make sure you do so wisely. I believe you need to be responsible not just as a Witch, but also as a decent human being.

Take responsibility for every word you put out there and every action you take. That includes magic as well as general manners. When you work magic, you are changing and manipulating energy, and you need to take responsibility for it. Your magic will affect someone: when you cast a pebble into a pool of water it creates ripples, just as your magic does when you cast a spell. Witchcraft is not a game.

Giving Thanks

Do not forget to say thank you—it is only good manners! If you are working a spell, then you are asking for something, whether it is from the Universe, the Divine, or any other form.

There is a current trend of "manifesting" that seems to be done by spiritual and non-spiritual folk alike. The whole idea is to ask for things, generally on a full moon. Sadly, what I have not seen in any of it is giving thanks. You cannot keep continually asking and taking; there must be some form of checks and balances.

When I work a spell asking for some help, guidance, or assistance, I always make sure to give an offering. An offering could be saying a simple thank you aloud, feeding the birds or watering the plants, pouring a libation of wine or bread onto the earth, or leaving an offering for deity on my altar. It can even be giving up your own time to help a friend or neighbour. No matter how you choose to give thanks, you must give something back in some form.

Don't take my word for it—give it a try! When you work a spell asking for something (because, let's face it, every spell is a request to receive, whether it is for healing, prosperity, love, protection, or another member of the band), try giving an offering as soon as you have worked the spell. If you called in deity to help, then make an offering to them. If you are asking for healing or prosperity, then give something in exchange: feed the birds or donate something to charity; be kind to everyone you meet when out and about; bring your neighbour's dust bins in off the kerb; help someone put their shopping into their car… You get the idea. Offerings can also be in the form of words, song, or dance. Write a poem for your deity, sing a song to the nature spirits in your garden, or be creative in another way.

Get into the habit of bringing about balance. When you ask for something in a spell, give something in return. In a way, it is a form of sacrifice, similar to what our ancestors did when they put in a request to the gods—although I wouldn't suggest throwing a goat on your altar!

"An It Harm None" Disclaimer

My original training in Witchcraft was Wicca. At the time, way before the internet, my only source of learning was books I could find in obscure occult stores, and these books were mostly Wicca. One of the first things I learnt about was the Wiccan Rede. "An it harm none, do what ye will" is a line from what is referred to as the Wiccan Rede; the full sentence reads, "Eight words the Wiccan Rede fulfill, An it harm none, do what ye will."[6] In fact, this is the last sentence in a whole script.

I used to add this line onto the end of my candle spells as a disclaimer. Why? Because of this example I was told: if you work a spell to bring money your way and you do not add the "harm none" disclaimer, then the money could end up coming to you as a result of someone dying and leaving you money in their will. Obviously, you want to avoid this kind of situation. So, for many years, I added this disclaimer to every spell, even after my journey took me away from Wicca.

Until I had a bit of a lightbulb moment.

People seem to use the term in situations that do not require it, and it does seem to be overused. It's even written at the end of some comments on social media, as if an offensive or rude comment is okay because "an harm none" was added to the end of it! I do believe the original meaning of this phrase was twisted or lost along the way.

However, back to my lightbulb moment. What if this disclaimer is actually hampering the energy of the spell? Think about it. Every single spell works by manipulating, moving, or transforming energy. Which means that at some point in the spell, someone is going to be affected by it.

Let's say you work a spell for success in a job interview, and the spell is successful. You got the job, but that means the other people that interviewed did not get it. As a result of you obtaining the position, other people have been "harmed" by not getting it. Even the smallest and most insignificant spell is going to send out ripples of energy that affect others. If you add "an it harm none" to the end of your job interview spell, then it could restrict the spell and stop it from working properly.

---

6. Robert Mathiesen and Theitic, *The Rede of the Wiccae: Adriana Porter, Gwen Thompson, and the Birth of a Tradition of Witchcraft* (Providence, RI: The Witches' Almanac, 2006).

Since that moment of realisation, I have stopped using the term in my spell work. If my intention is clear enough, then my spells will not leave a trail of misfortune behind them. By removing the disclaimer, hopefully I am allowing the energy to flow as it needs to, without any obstacles.

This is a choice you will need to make. Whatever you decide, remember that with magic comes responsibility.

Sacred Space

For me, my altar is a sacred space, a place to focus my devotions and work my magic. It is an ideal space to leave offerings to deity, spirit guides, and ancestors. It is also a good spot to sit in front of and meditate.

An altar is an excellent place to work your spells too. It does not need to be a grand affair dripping in sparkling ornaments and covered with candles, although if that suits you, then go for it! Your altar can be as simple as a candle and a vase on a shelf or windowsill. Work with the space you have available. Your altar's location will depend on your living situation too. If you prefer to keep things hidden away, then a tray that you can lift in and out of a cupboard works brilliantly. Your altar could be a shelf, a bookshelf, a tabletop, or the top of a sideboard. You can even work with a slab of wood or a flat stone in your garden.

An altar is very personal, so you need to place items on it that mean something to you. You might like to place ornaments that represent your deities and your spirit guides. Offering dishes and pentagrams can also go on your altar, along with representations of the four elements. And, as discussed in chapter 1, all of the elements can be represented by a candle!

If you have the space and the inclination, you might like to have several altars around the house for different purposes. Altars can also be dressed to represent the sabbats and the seasons. I have several altars. One is dedicated to my matron and patron deities. Another altar is my "working altar," where I do all my spell working. I also have an altar in the garden where I leave offerings to the spirit of place. Then I have a small altar on the corner of my dressing table, where I perform my morning devotions; this is very simple and has a candle for the Goddess, a candle for dragon energy, and a small statue of the Goddess.

You do not have to have an altar to be able to work with candle magic. Even though I have several altars, I often work spells just sitting at my kitchen table or out in the garden. Go with what works for you.

Casting a Circle

It is your choice whether you cast a circle before working a candle magic spell or not. The idea of casting a circle is to create protection, but also to show that the area within is sacred space. You don't necessarily need sacred space to work a spell; it is personal choice. If you are dealing with spirit, the world of fairy, or negative energies, then I would say it is a wise precaution. Otherwise, it is not necessary.

I start facing north and walk or visualise clockwise around in a circle until I am back facing north again. When I say a "circle," what is actually required is a sphere. Walking or visualising a circle around your space then needs to be added to. This can be done by visualising energy coming up from the circle and forming a dome above you as well as energy coming down from the circle and forming a dome below you. It can also be created by first walking your circle, then visualising energy above you from north to south and below you from east to west.

If you feel it is right to cast a circle, it does not have to be an elaborate ritual with quarter calling and bell ringing—a big ritual takes time and effort to plan and put together, and I don't feel it is necessary each time you work a spell. A circle ritual also usually calls upon the elements and deity, and you probably won't feel the need to include that in every spell. A basic protective circle will do the trick! It is quick and easy to work with and will still make you feel safe and secure in your work.

I do not often cast a circle when working a spell because my house is already protected to the hilt with boundary magic; I typically do not feel it is necessary to cast a circle. Keep in mind that I also work with ritual and magic regularly, so that protection has built up over time; as I have lived in my house for over twenty-six years, there is plenty of protection magic in place!

Practice

Basic Protective Circle

1. Walk deosil (clockwise) around the area you are going to be doing your working in.

2. Visualise a bright white light forming a circle around you.

3. Visualise the circle expanding above you to form a dome.

4. Visualise the circle expanding below you to complete the sphere.

5. When you have finished your working, walk widdershins (counter-clockwise) around the area, visualising the protective circle dissipating.

Working with Energy

For candle magic, you also need to know how to work with energy. Your candle and any ingredients you add to the spell working will need to be charged with the energy of your intent. To do this, you need to draw energy from around you: from the earth, the air, the sun, the moon, or the elements. Please never draw energy from within yourself—you will deplete your own reserves and exhaust yourself. Mother Nature has plenty of energy for us to use. Use your body as a channel for that outside energy: draw it through you and into the candle. I like to draw the energy from the earth beneath me, channelling it up through my legs and my torso, down my arms, and out through the palms of my hands and into the candle. As I do this, I also bring in my visualisation of the desired outcome.

The following sections detail a few other ways you can work with energy. Regardless of the method you choose, it helps to visualise your goal whilst you are raising the energy.

Drumming or Chanting

Drumming or chanting are both excellent ways of raising energy. Chanting the same phrase or words over and over raises energy; even a one-word chant said over and over again can raise energy that can be sent into your candle spell.

There will come a point with either of these where you feel a "high"—that means you have reached the peak of raising energy. Then you need to release that energy and send it where it needs to be.

For example, if you are raising energy to send it into a candle magic spell, at that "high" point, stop drumming or chanting and release the energy. Visualise it flowing from you and being directed into the candle.

Drawing Energy

Energy can be drawn directly from the sky, the sun, the moon, the earth, or the air around us without channelling it through your body. Direct the energy with your hands, as if you were herding it into the right place, or visualise the energy being sent directly into your target. For instance, with a candle spell, you could see energy flowing from the sun and hitting the candle like rays of light.

You can also "scoop up" the energy. Visualise energy flowing from the earth or the air. Scoop it up with your hands and pour it into the candle.

Practice

Energy Ball

To help you recognise and get the feel of energy, this is a neat little exercise. If you practice regularly, you will soon be working with energy without even thinking about it.

1. Sit quietly in a place where you won't be disturbed.

2. Begin by rubbing your hands together.

3. When the palms of your hands are warm, slowly pull your hands apart.

4. When your hands are a few inches apart, gently try and push them back together. At this point, you should feel a little resistance. This is energy that you have created out of the air, which has created a small energy ball between your hands.

5. To release the energy, throw the ball up into the air or clap your hands.

Practice

Channelling Energy

1. With both feet placed on the floor, begin by visualising energy flowing from the earth. See it being drawn up from earth's core, through the soil, and into your feet.

2. Allow that energy to flow up through your legs, through your torso, and down your arms. Then allow that energy to flow through your hands, and direct the energy out through your palms or fingertips.

This exercise can also be done by visualising a bright light. (It can be any colour you'd like. I usually work with white, but I tailor the colour to suit the spell's intent. For instance, I work with blue light for healing.) Allow this light to flow from the sun, moon, or sky and into the top of your head. Let the energy flow down through your neck, your torso, and your arms, finally leaving your body through your hands.

You could try drawing energy from the air around you. Visualise the air being sucked into your body directly, allowing it to flow through your arms and into your hands. Then, direct the energy where you need it to go by releasing it through your palms or fingertips.

Energy can also be drawn in from the air around you by taking deep breaths in, filling your body with that air energy. Then it can be channelled out through your body and hands to where it is needed. For spells where you need just a bit of energy, breathe the air energy in through your mouth and exhale it onto the candle or wherever you need it.

Visualisation

When working candle magic (or, indeed, any spell), one of the main tasks is to use visualisation skills. Some of you will already have mastered visualisation; for others, it may come naturally; for some, it will be a work in progress. Visualisation may require a bit of extra effort on your part. Super-sharp visualisation skills take practice!

Let me give you an example of using visualisation in a spell. Perhaps I need to bring in some more money to cover an unexpected bill. As I work my spell, I see in my mind's eye an image of me receiving money. I visualise someone handing me cash or see myself opening the post and receiving a cheque for the amount that I need.

Here is another example of using visualisation, this time in a healing spell. Let's say I have a friend who is feeling unwell. The image I create in my mind as I work the spell is of my friend. I visualise them feeling full of energy and in perfect health, able to get up from their sickbed and be full of life.

Visualisation is a little like daydreaming. I set the scene in my head and watch it play out, with the goal or desire happening as if it is a motion picture. However, I want to add a little disclaimer here: gaining this type of detailed visualisation skill can be difficult for some, and that is absolutely okay—it really is. Practicing visualisation exercises does help, but even then, not everyone is able to see a complete scene unfold. Don't be disheartened if you don't get a 360-degree, full-colour, high-definition visualisation—very few people do! Just visualising the general idea of what's happening or what needs to happen is all you need to do spell work.

Following is a visualisation exercise that can be adapted to suit any kind of magical practice. While I wrote it about a candle, you could visualise any object, such as an apple or a plant. Keep working with this exercise to increase your skill set. The idea is to hone your visualisation skill, so add to the visualisation each time you do this exercise to challenge yourself. Being able to visualise your goals and your completed desires really helps boost your magic.

Practice

Visualisation for Candle Magic

For this exercise, you will need a candle (it doesn't matter what size, shape, or colour) in a safe holder and a lighter or matches.

1. Sit quietly and set the candle in front of you. Light the wick.
2. Take a few deep breaths in and out. Focus on your breathing until you feel calm and centred.
3. Now look at the flame. Watch it move and notice all its colours. Next, take in the candle itself: the shape, the size, the colour.
4. Once you believe you have all the details locked in, close your eyes.

5. Try to recreate a detailed image of the candle in your mind's eye.
   Visualise the size, the shape, the colour, and the flame. Can you
   see the flame moving?

6. When you have had enough, slowly open your eyes and snuff out the
   candle.

You can recreate this exercise with any item, such as a piece of fruit or a
flower. It is the recreation of all the details that hones your visualisation skills.

Keep a Record

If you are proficient at journaling, then this practice will flow easily for you.
If, like me, you purchase numerous beautiful notepads with the intention of
keeping a record of all your thoughts and magical workings, write on the first
page, and then add it to the stack of abandoned notepads, this may be a little
more difficult, but keeping a record of your spells is worth the effort.

There are so many benefits to keeping a record. When you keep a record,
you note exactly what you used and did and when you did it. If you need to
work similar magic in the future, you can refer back to your record and tweak
a less-successful spell to improve it, or you can reuse a successful spell without
having to desperately try to remember what you did last time. Your record also
helps you monitor your success rate and failures, and it can help you figure out
why a spell didn't work for you. Some colours or herbs may work better for
you than others; keeping a record of them allows you to create your very own
reference guide. It also helps to have a record if you need to reverse a spell.

If you're not sure where to start when it comes to keeping a record, I suggest you write down the following for each spell:

+ Intent
+ Colour and type of candle(s) used
+ Date and time of working, including day of the week
+ Lunar phase and zodiac sign
+ Solar zodiac sign
+ Herbs used, if any, and the purpose or focus for each
+ Oils used, if any, and the purpose or focus for each

+ Crystals used, if any, and the purpose or focus for each
+ Any other items used, such as charms, pins, sigils, symbols, incense blends, etc.
+ Exact steps taken, in order
+ Exact words spoken
+ How long it took for the candle to burn out
+ Any specific or odd flame movements
+ The result of the spell and how long it took to work

Building Intent

Contrary to popular belief, most Witches don't work dozens of spells a week. Generally, the first step when faced with any issue or situation is to try and sort it out in a mundane way. Problem with a neighbour? Talk to them about it. Issue with bullying at school? Talk to the head teacher. Money problems? Take a proper look at your finances and note any way you can adjust spending or bring in more cash. Only once all the mundane avenues have been investigated would I then think about working a spell.

Before doing spell work, you must think about your specific need. As an example, when I first started on my magical journey, one of the first spells I worked was to get rid of any negative energy. I believed that all negative energy was bad and I didn't want it in my life, so I worked a banishing spell. There are two problems with this. Firstly, there is nothing that negative energy loves more than a void. I had created a void, so it did not take long for the negative energy to seep back into it. Secondly, nothing is ever as simple as negative or positive, black or white, good or bad. You need balance. A battery does not work with only positive energy—it needs the negative too. Life is pretty much the same.

Once I had worked my banishing spell, I found that friends were fading out, never to be seen again; people, groups, and options all disappeared from view. Why? Because most things have a bit of negative energy, and I had banished the whole lot! I had not been specific; I had not thought the whole situation through properly. Bad move.

Specificity applies to most spell intents, even with something like a money spell. You can ask that money comes your way, but if you do not think further than that, the money may flow right into your hands and then disappear just as quickly!

To avoid these types of pitfalls, I recommend sitting quietly and really thinking about your situation. What can you do to remedy it? What do you actually need? (This isn't always the same as what you want.) Remember that some situations may have underlying causes that you are not immediately aware of. Take some time to dig beneath the surface. Most situations are learning opportunities, if we want to see them that way. Don't immediately assume you need to banish something; maybe you just need to learn how to work with it, use it, or grow from it.

Before turning to spell work, reflect on your current situation. Read through the following questions and think carefully about your answers. I recommend grabbing your notepad and writing your answers down. Be totally honest with yourself.

- What do you really need in your life, in terms of material needs? Focus not on what you want, but what you really need.
- What would need to happen to secure your intent for the long-term? Think beyond the short-term.
- What do you have available to you now that you can utilise to put your goal into action in the real world?
- Do you want to change how you feel emotionally or spiritually? What is one step you can take to make that happen?
- If magic is the solution, what will you do in the mundane world to help back up your spell? Every spell needs support in real life. For example, you cannot work a spell to get a new job and then just sit back and wait for it to land in your lap; you would need to actively look for one!

If you're struggling to answer any of these questions, you could turn to a divination tool. Divination can help clarify things for you. Ask the question and draw a tarot or oracle card. You could even draw two or three cards as a reading if you'd like some direction on the spell you want to work. Tools like the ogham, a pendulum, or runes can be used in a similar way.

Practice

Mind Map for Intent

If you want to clarify your intent, you can make a mind map. A mind map is a way of organising your thoughts and honing your focus using a visual representation. It can help you bring structure to your spell (or any area of your life, really). A mind map is a diagram with a nonlinear layout; it spreads out from a central idea or theme. When you create a mind map, you basically dump all your ideas and thoughts onto paper. Then you can sort through what is important and relevant and what isn't.

1. Take a sheet of paper (or a blank page in one of those many empty notepads) and write your intent as one word in the centre of the page.

2. Now write words that are associated with your intent around the page. Do not think too hard about this; just write whatever pops into your head.

3. Once you feel you are finished, sit back and look at the words.

4. Draw lines from each word to the centre intent, or to each other.

5. What are the connections? Which words seem more important than the others?

Timing

When doing spell work, make sure to give your spell a time frame. Sharing how quickly you want things to happen helps guide the magic. I often have people tell me their spell has not worked, but they did not set a time frame— the spell may be working, just very slowly!

If you need something by a set date, make sure you include that in the spell. Even if you do not have a requirement date as such, I recommend including a set date so your spell has boundaries. Give the magic a reasonable deadline so it has time to get everything in order.

Speed Magic

It can be quite easy to slip into the habit of working magic as a quick fix. I will admit, I have worked magic on the fly before. Sometimes you need to utter an impromptu spell, such as a spell for protection when out and about or a quick chant to secure a parking space. But here is the thing: you do not want to rush spells if you can help it. Spells take time and effort to put together, and they should get your full attention and focus.

Even the most thought-out and carefully worked spell can veer off in an unexpected direction, so imagine what chaos can happen when a spell is worked in a rush! More than likely, quick spells will lead to putting out small fires rather than stopping the next problem before it happens. A spell worked in a hurry will only be a short fix—if it works at all.

Are you constantly working speed spells? If you are, nothing will ever be resolved. My advice is to stop and think before doing another quick spell. Really reflect on the situation; work through the questions shared earlier in this chapter. Take the time to treat your magic with care and respect.

Calling for Help

You can boost your magic by asking for assistance from deity or the Otherworld. Whenever you work with outside help, please do your research first. Get to know the entity you will be calling upon. (For example, you would not want to reach out to a war god for help with a love spell.) If you want to work with a deity, research their culture, their history, and their likes and dislikes. Then, build a relationship before asking for support; it's important to do the foundational work before asking deity for favours. And do not forget your manners! Remember to give thanks afterwards. Leaving an offering wouldn't hurt either.

If you're planning to ask a specific deity to lend their support to your spell, I recommend adding an image of them to your altar; this will help you focus. You could also add their favourite herbs and oils to help strengthen the connection. Spirit energy or deity can be called in at the beginning of a spell, or you can call them in as part of your chant.

Words, Chants, and Rhymes

You can add colours, herbs, symbols, and countless other layers to your spell, but ultimately, magic needs to be told what to do. This can be done verbally (words spoken aloud) or internally. If you need to be discreet, you can think the words silently, in your head. Try to mouth the words as you think them so that they are sent out into the world rather than just rattling around in your brain. Whether you say spells verbally or internally, the result will ultimately be the same. However, if you can say your spells aloud, it really helps solidify your intention and raise energy.

There are different ways you can direct your words; how you do so is up to you. If you're not sure where to start, I recommend speaking from the heart. State your intent aloud to the Universe, the Divine, and deity. Tell them exactly what you require in your own words. This is done in the form of a request, just like a conversation (albeit fairly one-sided).

Here are some other ways to verbalise your spells.

Chanting
Chanting is a repeated phrase that is kept simple but said over and over. Chanting often works well in a group and can raise a significant amount of energy.

Invocations
An invocation is an invitation. Invocations invite a power to direct their energy into a spell. Invocations can be directed towards deity or the elements, for instance.

Incantations
An incantation is a phrase that gives clear direction; it explains the purpose of a spell. This often comes in the form of a poem or a rhyme.

Repetition
Repeating a word or short phrase a certain number of times can add a magical layer to your spell. Numbers have magical intent. I often repeat a phrase or action in a spell three times, as three is a magical number, but you can tie any number to your intent as long as there is a reason behind it.

Psalms
Do not discount the use of Psalms in spell work. Psalms have been used in magic for thousands of years, often in the form of prayer healing or faith healing. The Book of Psalms are words written down that were originally spoken

as prayers and used in spell working. They were created before Christianity. In fact, a book of spells called the Heptameron is filled with spells using verses from Psalms that dates back to 1496. The Jewish Qabalah contains information on using Psalms for magic too. In the early 1800s, the magical practice known as Hoodoo emerged, with the inclusion of Psalms in some spell work.[7]

Rhyming

A question I am often asked is "Do the spell words need to rhyme?" My answer is always "No, they don't." So why is there such a focus on making spells rhyme? Well, rhyming does make spells sound more impressive. A rhyming spell feels like it is full of magic. In addition, rhyming can add to the power and focus of a spell; if you've made an effort to have the words rhyme, that means you have given significant time and energy to your spell.

Not everyone can string rhyming words together effortlessly—we're not all natural poets! If you struggle to think of rhyming words off the top of your head (as I often do), there are numerous websites that can provide them for you. Just type in the word you want a rhyme for and browse the various options.

Once you have your rhyming spell written out, test it by reading it aloud. Saying a spell aloud is an effective way of finding out whether it flows properly. Sometimes it looks good on paper but sounds a bit clunky in practice. If the spell doesn't sound quite right, try removing or adding a word until you find the right balance.

At the end of the day, your spells do not have to rhyme if that does not appeal to you. I believe that words said from the heart are clear and concise, and they can be just as powerful.

Using Pre-Written Spells

You do not need to create each spell from scratch. Using spells written by others is absolutely fine—that applies to spells found in books (including this one, obviously) and on the internet. In fact, pre-written spells give you a starting point, a good foundation to build upon, and, of course, inspiration. You could work a spell exactly as it was written, but I would encourage you to

---

7. Taren S, *Hoodoo in the Psalms: God's Magick* (Winchester, UK: Moon Books, 2019).

tweak it. If you do not have all the ingredients for the spell, determine what you can substitute. If the colours used do not feel right to you, change them. If the oils or herbs do not all seem to fit for you, switch them out for ones that do. Switch up the wording to add your own personal touch. Using spells written by others does work really well, but they work even better if you tweak them a bit to make them unique to you.

CHAPTER THREE

Beginning Candle Magic

Candle magic is one of the most useful types of magic and is incredibly easy to work with. In this chapter, I share the very basics to get you started. If you already work with candle magic, there are some suggestions to improve your practice as well. My hope is that after you read this chapter, you will experiment and find methods of candle magic that suit you and your type of magic. Don't hesitate to tweak the spells for your own purposes; the spell and intent may benefit from these variations!

A quick candle magic spell can be done by lighting a plain white candle and just asking for what you need. However, adding extra ingredients such as herbs and oils will bring extra layers of energy and power to your spell. If you are going to take the time to work some magic, why not make it worthwhile?

Selecting a Candle

Ultimately, the choice of candle is yours. It should be based on your intuition and, of course, your budget. See chapter 4 for detailed explanations of the different types of candles you could use in your magic. If you have an unlimited stash of candles of all kinds, then pick the candle that works best for your spell intent. If you only have a few candles, then lay them out in front of you and let your intuition guide you. If you only have one candle, then make it work for you by adding in other ingredients. There are no hard-and-fast rules!

As far as candle colour, coloured candles are excellent because they add a layer of energy to your spell. However, if all you have (or all you can afford) are plain white candles, those will work perfectly. Some coloured candles are only coloured on the outside: a white candle was dipped into a thin coating of coloured wax. For the purpose of spell work, I don't believe this matters too much; you may feel otherwise. Dipped coloured candles are generally cheaper than those that are coloured all the way through.

Cleansing a Candle

Before you use a new candle, it is beneficial to cleanse it. Cleansing clears up any bits of energy that the candle may have picked up on its journey to you. It is a bit of magical housekeeping to ensure no stray energy interferes with your magic. Cleansing a candle is simple and can be done via several methods; which one is up to you.

> **Visualisation:** Simple and effective. Hold the candle or set it in front of you and visualise a bright light. (The light could be clear, white, blue, or whatever colour you associate with cleansing.) See the light spreading over the candle, clearing and cleansing any negative energy.
>
> **Smoke:** Light some incense, then pass your candle through the smoke. Choose a scent that you associate with cleansing and purifying; suggestions include garden sage, mint, or mugwort. See the smoke clearing away any negative energy that may be stuck to the candle.
>
> **Water:** Pass the candle briefly under running water, or sprinkle it with blessed or moon water. Visualise any negative energy being washed away as you do so.
>
> **Crystals:** If you have a large cluster quartz or rose quartz, you can place the candle on top and leave it overnight to cleanse. Alternatively, take a piece of quartz, rose quartz, selenite, or black obsidian and run the crystal over the candle, circling it counterclockwise around the candle to dispel any negative energy. See the crystal energy clearing any negative energy that may have held onto the candle.

Charging a Candle

Once your candle is cleansed, you need to charge it with positive energy. This can be done in several ways.

Moonlight: Leave your candle in the moonlight for a few hours. You can tie this to the intent of your spell work if you know what you are going to use the candle for; charge the candle under a new moon for magic to draw something to you, a waning moon for releasing magic, or a full moon for general spells.

Sunlight: If you want to draw on solar energy for your magic, you can charge the candle in sunlight. Leave the candle under the midday sun for a few minutes before using it in general spells. (Don't leave a candle out in full sun for too long—it may melt!) If you are working magic to draw something to you, charge the candle for a few minutes at sunrise or mid-morning; for releasing magic, charge it under the afternoon sun or sunset.

Visualisation: Hold the candle in your hands and visualise your intent filling the candle. Or, just channel sun, earth, or element energy into the candle.

Crystals: If you have a large piece of quartz of any kind, you can set the candle on top of the crystal and leave it to charge. I like to leave them overnight, but be guided by how long *you* feel the candle needs to charge.

Charging Ingredients

After cleansing and charging the candle with positive energy, you must tell your candle and any other ingredients what you want them to do. You need to programme your items so they have a direction and purpose. I do this with all the items in every spell I am working.

Start with the candle. It may be charged with positive energy, but it still needs to be told what intent you have in mind. Hold the candle in your hands and channel energy into it whilst visualising your intent (exercises for both can be found in chapter 2). Follow this same process with any other ingredient you want to add to the spell. (One exception is essential oil, which I charge while I am dressing the candle.)

For each herb, spice, or crystal I use in a spell, I hold it in my hand and channel energy with my intent while I tell it what I want it to do. You can even give the ingredients your instructions out loud. For example: "Basil herb,

I charge you with the intent of drawing money to me." Later, visualise your goal or desire when you add the ingredient to the spell. All herbs, spices, and crystals have magical energy, but most of them are correspondences for several different things, so they need your guidance to give them focus and direction.

Dressing a Candle

To add even more power to your candle spell's intent, you can add scent, either in the form of anointing the candle with oil or rolling it in herbs. Suggestions for corresponding herbs and oils can be found in chapter 6.

Warning: Adding oils and herbs to your candles can cause the candle flame to flare. Try to keep any oils or herb dressings away from the wick. Dried herbs and oils are combustible and can send the flame of your candle sky high; they can also cause spitting. Be mindful of this when setting your candle spell in motion. Keep it in a fireproof holder on a safe surface and watch it like a hawk! Trust me, I speak from experience, and I have the scorched furniture to prove it. Thankfully, my eyebrows are still intact.

Anointing with Oil

Anointing means to rub or dab with oil for a religious or spiritual purpose. You can dab anointing oils on your pulse points to help you tap into your spiritual self. However, in this section, I'm focusing on anointing candles with an oil blend to dedicate them for a specific purpose. When you anoint a candle, you direct energy and intent to your spell work. In the case of dedication candles, anointing guides the energy to the deity or spirit.

Whilst you are anointing your candle with oil and/or rolling it in herbs, it is important to visualise your intent at the same time. By "charging" the herbs and oils as you add them to the candle, you are adding even more power to your spell.

Here are a few different ways to anoint a candle. The following exercises are for use with spell, taper, or pillar candles, or any candle that has an exposed column.

Practice

Dressing a Candle to Bring Something to You

1. Rub oil from the bottom of the candle up to the centre.

2. Rub oil from the top of the candle down to the centre.

3. Rub the oil from the top of the candle right to the bottom. This can be done with the candle standing upright, or you can hold the candle horizontally with the wick pointing away from you so that when you dress it from top to bottom, you are bringing the energy towards you.

4. Rub the oil clockwise in a spiral from the top of the candle to the bottom.

Practice

Dressing a Candle to Dispel or Send Away from You

1. Rub the oil from the centre to the top.

2. Rub the oil from the centre of the candle to the bottom.

3. Rub the oil from the bottom of the candle right to the top. This can be done with the candle standing upright, or you can hold the candle horizontally with the wick facing you so that when you dress it from bottom to top, you are sending the energy away from you.

4. Rub the oil counterclockwise in a spiral from the bottom of the candle to the top.

Oil blends can also be inserted into the base of a candle. Use a bradawl, skewer, or screwdriver to carve out a small hole, then push the oil mixture inside.

Anointing a Contained Candle

If your candle is in a container and slides out, remove the wax and dress it with oil as in the previous exercises.

For candles set in containers, you can add an oil blend on the top of the wax. Do not be heavy-handed with this, as too much oil could cause the flame to flare or the glass to crack.

If you are anointing a tea light candle, you have a few options. You could add a few drops of your chosen oil and a sprinkle of herbs on top. Some tea light candles slide out of their metal tin, so you could dress the candle like normal and then slip it back into the tin. Another option would be to sprinkle drops of oil or herbs in the base of the tin before popping the candle back in.

Anointing a Shaped Candle

When anointing seven-knob candles or shaped candles, you can get creative. Dress each knob, side, or part of the shape with different oil blends to correspond with your spell. Shaped candles with eyes, hands, or feet can be used for specific intents or influences in the spell. For example, a foot-shaped candle could be dressed for use in a grounding spell; an eye-shaped candle could be used for psychic abilities, clarity, or seeing the truth in a situation.

Adding Herb and Spices

Once anointed with oil, you can roll your candle in crushed herb or spice blends. The oil helps the herbs stick to the wax of the candle. There are a few caveats to this:

- If you are using a rolled beeswax candle, you can warm the wax in your hand and gently unroll the beeswax, sprinkle herbs inside, and roll it back up again.
- If you have a glass votive holder, you can place the candle inside and sprinkle herbs or spices around it.
- For large pillar candles, you can sprinkle a mixture of dried herbs or spices on top. Be careful not to place them too near the wick! You can seal the herbs or spices in place by holding a lighted taper candle over the pillar candle and allowing the taper's melting wax to drip on top.
- Whole pieces of cinnamon stick can be placed around the sides of pillar candles and tied in place with a ribbon.
- Cloves can be pushed into the sides of candles.

Decorating and Adorning Candles

Adding your own embellishments to a candle not only makes it look pretty (or Witchy), but also adds magic and power. You can decorate a candle based on your personal decoration preferences, or you can choose ingredients intuitively. You can also adorn a candle with correspondences (such as pressed flowers and leaves, colourful glitter, essential oils, crystal chips, or charms) with your particular intent in mind. Please do be careful with these—oils and dried plants can cause flames to flare up, and crystals and charms can get incredibly hot—and even explode. Heat can also cause glass or ceramic holders to crack. It is advisable to remove crystals, large flowers, and leaves as the wax melts, just to be safe; the magical energy will remain the same.

Here are some of my favourite methods to decorate and adorn my candles.

Pressed Flowers or Leaves
Melt a little candle wax. Using a small paintbrush, dip into the melted wax and brush a small amount onto the back of the flower or leaf, then press it onto your candle. Once you are finished adding your flowers and leaves, brush a light layer of melted wax over the top to seal them in.

Wax Painting
Melt small amounts of coloured candle wax. Using a small paintbrush, dip into your colours and paint an image onto the candle. This method also works well if you have a stencil.

Crystals
Small crystal chips can be added to the top of large pillar candles. I put the chips on top and then hold a lighted taper candle over the top, allowing the melting wax to drip over the top of the crystal chips and seal them in.

Larger crystals and tumbled stones set around a candle can lend energy to it. Small crystals can be pushed into the base of candles to support your intent, and if a small crystal is pushed into the centre of a candle, it focuses energy on the intent of the spell.

Another option is to place one crystal in front of the candle to absorb the energy of the spell. The crystal can then be carried with you or placed on your altar.

Thorns
Thorns from plants such as blackthorns and roses can be used instead of pins in candle magic, or they can be pushed into the sides for decoration. Using thorns adds to a spell's magical properties and brings in the earth element.

Charms

Small metal charms can be added to candles. These can be sealed on top of a pillar candle in a similar way to crystal chips and herbs, or you could pin them onto the side of candles.

Ribbons

Colourful ribbons can be tied around the middle of candles. For extra magic, charms can be tied to the ribbons first. Remember to remove the ribbon(s) before burning the candle.

Personal Items

To connect a candle to you or another person, add something personal. Nail clippings or a piece of hair are easy to add to a candle; just push them into the top of the candle and seal with extra wax. I recommend doing this if you are working a spell for yourself or a friend, particularly if the spell is for healing. These items are deeply personal, and they create a very strong connection indeed. Of course, this same idea also applies if you are working a spell to curse someone.

Photographs and Images

A small photograph can be pinned to a candle to connect it to the person the magic is intended for, or it can be placed underneath the candle. If your candle is in a container, you can stick the photograph to the outside.

Alternatively, cut images from magazines or find some online and print them out, then pin or stick them to your candle. Create a spell "place mat" with images that represent your wishes and place it underneath your candle. For example, printed images of money can be used in money-drawing spells, and a candle spell for a new car could include an image of the exact make and model you desire.

Once you've lit the candle, be mindful of any photos burning—you may want this to happen as part of your spell, but be careful and keep an eye out for any flames or fumes this may cause.

Shaping

If you are feeling artistic, it is possible to carve a candle into another shape. Using a sharp knife, carefully sculpt a candle into the shape you desire. Make sure you leave enough wax around the central wick. You could carve candles into spheres, pyramids, cubes, or even crosses.

Lighting a Candle

It might seem strange to spend time talking about how to light a candle. Surely it is a simple action? Well, yes and no. Practically, it is: you could use matches, a lighter, or a taper. Magically, there is a bit more to it.

If you light a candle using a match, this adds the magical element of wood and a striking action. I like to save my spent matches so I can use them in magic as a form of charcoal; you can grind them up and add the powder to spells, or you can draw sigils and symbols with the blackened end. A lighter works too; it does not have quite the same energy, but it still has the element of fire within it. If you have several candles to light, I think it is easier to use a lighting taper or wooden spill to pass the flame on. Think about your options, then make a decision about which method you prefer.

When to light a candle is also a choice you need to make. Do you light the candle before or after you start your spell? Lighting the candle at the beginning of the spell tells the Universe that are you setting things in motion, and it can also focus you and set the mood. Lighting the candle during the spell (perhaps once you start your chant or speak your words of intent) also works; this sets magic in motion and does so with your words. Candles can also be lit at the end of a magical working; this sends the energy out into the world. Personally, I nearly always light my candles at the beginning of a spell, but the choice must be yours. What feels right for you?

Snuffing a Candle

There is controversy around whether you should blow out a candle or snuff it (either with your fingers or a candle snuffer). Some say that you should never blow out a candle flame, believing this severs the connection between the magic and the Divine, or that it insults the element of fire. I have never had a problem and blow out candles when necessary, but I have a candle snuffer that I use on occasion too. Trust your intuition on this one. It may help to cup your hand behind the candle when you blow the flame out; this helps keep the magic "contained." Bear this in mind: when blowing out a candle, blow lightly, or you could send hot wax in unexpected directions!

I typically allow a candle to burn down fully when working a spell unless it is a seven-day spell or a pinned one. I feel that the candle needs to burn fully to allow the magic to be released properly. On occasion, you may feel that a candle has done its work even when it has only burned halfway through, or when it has burned past an inscription or carving. In that case, it can be snuffed or blown out and the remains can be disposed of.

If you do not have time to let a candle burn down fully, one option is to set a burn-time limit. Use a number that corresponds with your spell intent, or choose a magical number. Be sure to choose a number that is in line with your purpose.

Using a candle snuffer is an effective way to pause a spell that you will come back to; it does not seem as abrupt or final as blowing it out. Allow your intuition to guide you to the best course of action.

When working with reversing spells or sending negative energy away, you can quickly turn a lit candle upside down to put the flame out. Turning a candle upside down reverses energy. Be careful, as this will send hot wax everywhere; placing something underneath to catch the wax is advisable. You can also upturn a lit candle and then extinguish it by turning it in water, soil, or sand. This is a way of requesting that Mother Earth absorb the negative energy.

Dancing Flames

Once lit, how a candle's flame moves can be an indication of how a spell is working. I say "can" because other factors come into play. Check that there is not a draught affecting the movement of the flame. Even your breath can move the flame if you are close. The quality of the materials used in the candle and any added correspondences can also affect how the flame moves. In other words, check for mundane reasons before assuming there are magical reasons.

If you have ruled out any external influences affecting the flame, then tap into your intuition and see what conclusions you can draw. Here are some of my interpretations.

Jumping Flame

If the flame is all over the place, jumping and dancing about, it could mean the spell will struggle against opposition and blockages. It can also indicate anger is involved in the situation somehow.

Flickering Flame

If the flame is flickering slightly (rather than dancing about), it may mean that spirits are near. If you feel that is the case, you can ask if they have a message for you. A flickering flame can also foretell changes are about to happen.

High Flame

A candle spell with a high-burning flame is a positive sign. It could mean the spell will work quickly. Be wary, though—a high flame indicates success, but the results may not be long-lasting. In a cleansing or banishing spell, a long, high flame can indicate that the spell has a lot to work through!

Low Flame

If the flame is low burning, it could mean that the magic is struggling to fight against opposition or a blockage. You may need to work some extra magic to move the spell forward.

Goes Out

If the flame goes out completely before the candle has burned fully, it could mean the spell has failed, or it is not the right time to work that type of magic. The flame going out is not a positive sign. If this happens, dispose of all the ingredients and rethink your spell and intent.

White Smoke

If the candle produces white smoke, your spell should be successful, but you may encounter some difficulties before you reach your desired outcome.

Black Smoke

Black smoke can signify the presence of negative energy in the form of blockages. It could even mean that the spell needs to be stopped and the candle disposed of. Trust your intuition on this one. If you get a negative feeling when you see the smoke, snuff the candle out straightaway and dispose of the items. If you only get a small amount of black smoke initially and then it clears, this could mean the energy was struggling against negative vibes but has managed to clear them.

Burn Rates

In addition to monitoring a candle's flame and smoke, pay attention to its burn rate. Bear in mind that this may be affected by the type of wax and wick used, but burn rates can also indicate the likelihood of a spell's success.

Slow Burning

If a candle takes longer than expected to burn down, it could mean that the spell has a low chance of success. It could also mean that the spell will work, but will take a long time to come into effect.

Fast Burning

If the candle burns really quickly, it could mean the spell will be an enormous success and that everything will come to fruition in a timely manner. Be wary, though; a fast-burning candle could also indicate that although the spell is a success, its results will not be long-lasting.

Strong and Steady

If the candle is burning well and as you would expect it to, then your spell is working.

Not Properly Burned

If your candle does not burn properly or fully, or if it only burns on one side, then you may need to take another look at the intent of your spell. Perhaps your intent was not clearly stated, or maybe it is not right for the type of goal you are working towards.

Ending a Spell

How do you know when a spell is finished and has worked its magic? There is no straightforward answer, but here are some possibilities.

- You will intuitively know when the spell is done. You will get a feeling in your gut and just know that it is time to dismantle the spell or snuff the candle out.

- The spell may be finished when a candle burns itself out, when any pins used drop out, or when the candle burns down past any carvings or symbols.

- If you set a specific time frame for your spell to take effect, such as a week or a month, then the spell should be finished at the end of that time. Although, in this instance, I would consider it a judgement call—spirit and the Universe don't always work on the same timeline as we do.

- If you worked your spell under a particular moon phase, the spell may finish when that phase is over.

- Of course, the end of a spell could be your goal being reached. Perhaps the money you asked for comes in, or your healing spell worked and your loved one is feeling better.

The ending will be different for each spell. Keep in mind that some spells run out of steam before they have even come to fruition. If you suspect that is the case, give your spell a boost. Try adding a dash of essential oil, sprinkle some herbs, or relight the candle. Let your intuition guide you.

Disposing

When it comes time to dispose of spell remnants (which could be anything from a small candle stub or a few herbs right up to a whole poppet or jar), there are a few options. I've divided this section by item.

Candle Stubs and Wax Remnants

I generally dispose of these in the trash, although they can also be buried. Candle leftovers can be buried in garden soil, at a crossroads, or in the woods. Only do this if you are certain an item is biodegradable and does not contain lots of salt, as that is bad for the soil and for animals. You can also throw candle remnants into running water, such as a river or the sea. Again, please only do this if the items are not going to damage the environment or the wildlife.

If you're feeling crafty, wax remnants can also be used as charms or talismans (see chapter 5).

Herbs and Spices

If your remnants are just herbs and spices, these can be popped into the compost bin if you have one. Otherwise, I often sprinkle them straight onto the garden, particularly any ash in my cauldron, as some plants like this added to the soil. Remember: if you sprinkle herb and spice remnants that contain seeds onto the soil, they may grow!

One of my favourite ways to dispose of herbs and spices is to burn them! I do like a bit of fire. Herbs, spices, wood, and paper can all easily be burnt in a fireproof container after the spell is done. I know this may seem obvious, but please do not add anything to the flame that will produce toxic fumes.

Ash and dried herbs and spices can be thrown into the air on a windy day. But do remember that at some point, they will settle on the ground—or on you.

If I have used plant material in a candle spell grid, I often tip all the spices and herbs into a jar and label it with the spell's intent. Later, I use the mixture as loose incense in line with the intent of the original spell. As an example, if I have worked a prosperity spell, I will keep the herb mixture as incense and burn it when I work a future prosperity spell.

Crystals

If I use crystals in a spell, I cleanse them and then put them away for future use. Crystals are easy to clear with incense smoke, water, or salt, depending on the type of crystal. Crystals are expensive, so I do not throw them away after each spell.

Poppets

I tend to create poppets with an intent. I have one for prosperity; I write my need/want on a slip of paper and tie it to the poppet. When the spell is done, I burn the slip of paper and cleanse the poppet with incense so I can reuse it in future money spells. Those little guys take time to make, and I do not want to keep remaking them.

If you create a poppet for a specific person or for a curse, though, I would dispose of it afterwards. Toss it in the trash or burn it (if the materials are natural).

Binding Ingredients

If I have worked a binding spell, then I do not want that magic on my property once the spell is done. Even if the items are biodegradable, I do not chuck them on my garden. You do not want that energy anywhere near your house! Binding ingredients go into the trash to be taken far away.

Tea Light Tins and Other Candle Containers

Candle containers can be thrown in the trash, recycled, or saved to reuse: they can be refilled with new wicks and freshly melted wax. I clean them with soapy water before reuse.

Other Ingredients

Some items can be flushed down the toilet, such as liquids like water. I don't like flushing herbs, wax, and other items down the toilet. It can harm wildlife or the water source it will eventually end up in. Doing this can also clog the toilet pipes, which is definitely something to be avoided. If in doubt, use the trash bin.

Materials that are hazardous or nonbiodegradable (such as those that might be in a witch bottle or jar spell) should be dumped in the trash. Also remember that even once you throw the items in the trash, they will end up in the earth at a landfill. Think about the materials you are using in your spells. Try and keep as much of your practice as possible eco-friendly or reusable.

One important note: spells have the potential to go "off the rails," especially love spells. I always advise keeping some remnants of a spell—along with a list of exactly what you did and used—just in case you need to reverse it.

Ultimately, trust your intuition during the disposal process. Hold the remnants in your hand or hold your hand over the top of them and ask, "What do I do with these now?" See how you feel.

Reusing Candles

I do not reuse candles if I have previously worked with them in a spell. If the candle has only burned down partway and been snuffed out, I dispose of the remainder. Reusing a candle can confuse the energy. But remember, what works for me may be different than what works for you.

If you have leftover stubs from candles used for general lighting purposes or other mundane reasons, you can save them for reuse. When you have collected a few, melt them all together and make new candles out of the wax. I only do this with candle stubs that have not been used for spell work.

Deconsecrating

If you have used a candle for a working and have gone through the process of consecrating and charging it but now no longer need it, or if you have finished a spell and still have a large candle left, you can deconsecrate it. This will strip the candle of the spell's magic, allowing you to reuse it for something else. This process also works for poppets, talismans, and any other magical items. All you need are the item to be deconsecrated and some incense.

Focus on the object and visualise it surrounded by coloured light, a colour that represents in the intent it was used for. (For example, if it was a money spell, you might see the candle surrounded by a dark green light.) Then visualise the colour slowly fading from the light, losing saturation until it is white.

Light incense and hold the object in the smoke. Say a few words, such as: "I hold this candle in the cleansing smoke. It no longer has power, and the magic is relinquished. It is no longer needed to work a spell; it is now just an object, plain and simple. All energies are now released." I know that is not very poetic, but it does the job.

Your candle or other object is now de-magicked and can be used for another purpose.

Undoing or Reversing a Candle Spell

Sometimes a spell goes horribly wrong, or it was worked in the heat of anger. It happens! Here are a few pointers to avoid spell catastrophes:

- Do not work a spell if you are really angry or upset. Wait until you have calmed down and thought it through properly.

- Do not work a spell if you are drunk or high. Who knows what chaos you could cause!

- Keep detailed descriptions of your spells. Write down what you did, how you did it, when you did it, and what you used—if you have all this information on hand, it makes a spell easier to undo.

- Keep your spell remnants if the working has a possibility of going wrong, particularly in the case of bindings and love spells. If you have the remnants of a working, it will be easier to cancel out the original spell.

- Spells to break a hex, unbinding spells, and spells to remove curses can be adapted or used to undo a spell (particularly unbinding spells).

Here are some more ideas for undoing spells. Read through them all to see which tactic best fits your situation and the type of spell you worked.

Using Remnants

If you kept spell remnants from the spell you want to undo, you can simply burn them. This will cancel out the original spell perfectly. Note: This only really works if you did not use fire in the original spell casting. If you used fire initially, burning the remnants could *increase* the energy of the spell, and you really do not want to be doing that.

Using Details

If you wrote down specific details when you cast the spell you want to undo, you can work a new spell to cancel each step. Beside each step, each chant, and each ingredient used, make a note of the opposite.

For example, if you used a white candle in the original spell, use a black one in the new spell; if you used a purple candle, use a yellow one. (Reference a colour wheel to find the opposite colour if you are not sure.) If you used moon water in your original spell, you could replace that with sun water or fire. If you used an earth element, replace that with the air element some-how. Any herbs you used will need to be replaced with an opposing herb. Any words you used will need to be rewritten to have a cancelling effect. You might also like to work your reversing spell in the opposite order of the original. Think "opposites and reversing" for all the steps and ingredients.

Cord Cutting

Cutting cords works well if you have bound yourself to someone or something only to discover that the situation is now overwhelming, and you want out.

Cord cutting can be easily done with visualisation. Light a candle and ground and centre yourself. Then close your eyes and see yourself and the other person. Notice all the cords attaching you two together. There may be one main cord, or there might be several. Then you need to visualise each cord cutting and breaking away so that you ultimately have no cords connecting you. Finish the visualisation by saying something like "I cut the cords that bind us, I release the strings that connect us, I set both of us free." Snuff out the candle.

You might want to work some self-care after a cord cutting. Remind your-self that you are surrounded by love and happiness.

Stop the Magic

A simple "stop the magic" spell can also be used. Light a black candle and "see" the spell you worked. Then, snuff out the black candle and snap it in half. As you do so, visualise the original spell falling apart and breaking, dissipating into mist. You could accompany this by verbalising which spell you want to stop and cancel. Bury the broken candle or throw it in the trash.

Do Not…

Whatever you do, please do not use mirror magic or any kind of reflecting spell to undo one of your spells. Because you were the original person that cast the spell, the magic will bounce right back and hit you squarely in the face. I am quite sure that isn't what you want.

Protection

Do not forget that protection magic has an important place in all of this too. Keep your protective guard up to minimise any stray backlash. See chapter 12 for some examples of protection spells.

CHAPTER FOUR

Choosing a Candle

Candle magic can be worked with one simple candle, but which type? There is no straight answer to that question, because it all depends on what type of spell you want to work, whether you want to add in correspondences, and, of course, what you have on hand (or what is within budget). The good news is that candle magic is very adaptable. Spells can be worked with any type of candle, from a tiny birthday cake candle to a tall pillar.

In this chapter, I share a wide variety of candle types and purposes. Each candle type lends itself to different spell workings. With that being said, remember that this is just a guide. As always, trust your intuition; ask yourself which type of candle you feel is the right one to use.

Before we begin, a few more candle disclaimers. Remember that candles must not be left unattended. For candle magic, it is often best to use a candle that will burn out quickly, unless the candle is part of a spell that will be activated over a period of time. In most cases, tea lights work well, as do votives, small beeswax candles, and birthday cake candles. However—and here is where I am going to be contrary—ten-centimetre spell candles are the perfect choice for most spell work. They do not burn for hours, and they can get the magic done.

If you are doing a spell that has a major intent, you may want to invest more time and energy into working it. This is when size really does matter. For something very important, I lean towards seven-day candles or something larger, like a taper/dinner candle. I might even use a pillar candle and spread the spell over several weeks. Again, use your judgement. Think about your intent and determine which candle type would work best for your intended outcome.

Types of Candles

In this section, I discuss many different types of candles and include suggestions for how and when to use them.

Spell or Chime Candles

I know this type of candle as a *spell candle*, but they are also referred to as *chime candles*. They are small, slim candles, generally about 10 centimetres (4 inches) tall and 1½ centimetres (½ inch) in diameter. They burn for about an hour. They are called chime candles because they are used in angel or Christmas chimes; the flickering of the candle flame moves the small fan of the mechanism.

These are my go-to candles for working spells due to the range of colours they are available in, their convenient size, and their quick burn time. Spell candles are readily available in occult stores and online.

  • Best used for spells

BENEFITS OF SPELL OR CHIME CANDLES

  • Easy to dress in oil and herbs
  • Do not take too long to burn
  • Can be easily pinned
  • Come in a variety of colours
  • Can be carved/inscribed
  • Can be used as a poppet to represent a person

Practice

New Beginnings Candle Spell

Spell candles are useful for all kinds of intent. This spell focuses on new beginnings and can be used in many variations: for a new job, a new way of living, a new project or venture, and more.

You will need

> Green spell candle
>
> Lighter or matches
>
> Olive oil
>
> Geranium essential oil
>
> Sesame seeds
>
> Candleholder
>
> Knife or needle for carving
>
> Green leaf
>
> Pen
>
> The Fool tarot card
>
> Malachite tumbled stone

Charge all your items with the intent of new beginnings and opportunities. Then, prepare your candle whilst visualising the new pathway or new beginnings you are welcoming into your life.

Using a knife or needle, carve the symbol of an arrow into the side of the candle. I carve the arrow facing upwards for positive energy, but be guided by your intuition.

Mix a few drops of geranium essential oil into some olive oil. Dress the candle, bringing the oil towards you to invite new energy into your life.

Roll the dressed candle in sesame seeds and set it safely in a candleholder.

Take the green leaf and write "new beginnings" on it with a pen. Place the leaf under the candleholder if this can be done safely, or just set the leaf in front of it.

Place the Fool tarot card behind the candle, propped up if possible and facing you.

Place the malachite tumbled stone in front of the candle.

Light the wick and sit quietly, watching the candle flame. Keep visualising your goal. After a few moments, say:

> *Colour of green, fresh and bright*
> *Open up new beginnings and make it right*
> *Fertile seeds bring all things new*
> *A fresh start now, and help me find my way through*

Watch the flame and keep visualising your goal. Listen for any intuitive messages and take note of any symbols.

Allow the candle to burn out completely. Then, bury the leaf petition in soil. The malachite tumbled stone can be carried with you to keep the energy of new beginnings flowing. The tarot card can be left on your altar until the spell has worked, or you can place it back in the pack straightaway—trust your intuition on this.

Birthday Cake Candles

Birthday cake candles are excellent for working quick spells, as they come in all sorts of colours and burn out in a very short time. Measuring around 7 centimetres (2¾ inches) in height and 0.8 centimetres (¼ inch) in diameter, they do not stand on their own, so you will need to push them into clay or something similar. Birthday cake candles can be purchased at a wide variety of stores.

+ Best used for spells

BENEFITS OF BIRTHDAY CAKE CANDLES

+ Burn very quickly
+ Come in a variety of colours

Practice

Birthday Cake Candle Spell for Luck

Birthday cake candles are useful for fast spells, like when you need a little bit of luck in a hurry.

You will need

Green birthday candle

Candleholder

Lighter or matches

Slip of paper

Green pen

Lay the spell ingredients in front of you and charge the candle with your intent.

Take the slip of paper and, using the green pen, draw a four-leaf clover in the centre. Write the word "luck" on the paper three times. As you do this, visualise yourself being lucky and reaching your desired outcome.

Put the paper underneath the candleholder or in front of it.

Set the birthday candle in the holder, then light the candle.

Watch the candle flame as you continue to visualise your goal.

Once the candle has burned out, fold up the petition paper and pop it in your purse, wallet, or bag. Keep the petition there until the magic has worked or until you feel it needs renewing.

Tea Lights

Tea lights are commonly used in magic. A tea light is wax and a wick held in a small metal tin. They come in a variety of colours, and in different scents too. They usually burn for around four hours. You can sprinkle herbs or essential oils on top of them or draw sigils on the base of the tin. They measure just under 4 centimetres (1½ inches) in diameter and 2 centimetres (¾ inch) in height. Tea lights are available at a wide variety of stores and often come in packs.

- Can be used for spells, but are best for candle and crystal grids, in storm lanterns, and as altar candles

BENEFITS OF TEA LIGHTS

- Inexpensive to purchase
- Can be personalised by adding herbs or oils to the top
- Sigils can be drawn on the base of the tin
- The candle can be lifted out so that small petitions or herbs can be placed in the tin, with the candle then replaced on top
- Stand on their own, without the need for a holder (although I would recommend setting something heatproof underneath if using on furniture, as the tin gets hot)

Practice

Tea Light Candle Spell for Peace

Tea lights work well in grids and lend themselves to spell workings that take a bit of time and patience, such as a spell for peace.

You will need

    2 tea light candles

    Lavender essential oil

    Lighter or matches

    Dried thyme

    Marker pen

Set your ingredients out in front of you and charge the candles, oil, and herb with your intent.

Slip the candle out of the metal container. Using your marker pen, draw a circle inside each container, then slip the candle back in.

Put two drops of lavender oil on the top of each tea light. As you do, say:

Lavender to bring peaceful energy

Put a pinch of dried thyme on the top of each tea light and say:

Thyme, bring your magic of peace

Light the candles. Sit and watch the flames while visualising a peaceful and calming energy surrounding you and filling your space.

Tea lights take a while to burn, so I like to sit with them for a while before snuffing them out. I relight them the next day and keep doing so until they have burned out. I recommend lighting them before you start your day or at the end of the day, as this brings peace to you and your home.

Votives

A votive is a small candle about 4.8 centimetres (2 inches) tall and 4.6 centimetres (1¾ inches) in diameter. The word *votive* means giving a vow or a wish, often as a devotion or in gratitude. These candles come in all sorts of colours and scents. They stand on their own or can be dropped into glasses or jars. Dress them in oils and herbs for extra magical energy. Votives burn for up to fifteen hours; I don't often use votives for spell work since they take so long to burn. However, they are excellent candles to light regularly in honour of deity or as general altar candles. Votives are readily available for purchase online and in a variety of stores.

  + Best used for altar candles

Benefits of Votives
  + Come in a variety of colours
  + Come in a variety of scents
  + Stand on their own without the need for a holder
  + Can be used as a poppet to represent a person

Practice

Votive Candle Spell for Change

One of the only certainties in life is change. Sometimes change is welcome, maybe even necessary. Other times we are forced into change. Whichever way it happens, candle magic can help speed up change and/or help you deal with its effects.

You will need

Orange votive candle (ideally cinnamon scented; otherwise, add a pinch of ground cinnamon to the top)

White votive candle

Candleholders

Lighter or matches

Image that represents where you are now

Image that represents where you want to be[8]

Charge the white votive candle to represent where you are now. Charge all the other items, including the orange votive, with your intent and where you want to be in the future.

Set both candles in front of you, the white one to your left and the orange one to your right. Prop the image that represents you now behind the white candle and the image of where you want to be behind the orange candle. Prop them up if possible, and set them facing you.

Light the white one and say:

> *Candle white that is the past*
> *Help me make these changes last*
> *Now I let go of the old*
> *To move forward and be bold*

Sit quietly and watch the flame. Visualise all that you want to release. Let go of anything that is holding you back from making changes in your life. Visualise that which no longer serves you melting away.

When you feel ready, take the white candle and light the orange one using its flame. Then snuff out the white candle flame.

Watch the flame from the orange candle and say:

> *Time to move forward to make a change*
> *Help guide and support me in this range*
> *Transitions and changes now to make*
> *Let go and release, old habits to break*

---

8. The images could be photographs of yourself, physical places, or anything that represents your goal.

Spend some time watching the flame of the orange candle. Visualise changes and transitions happening smoothly. See yourself moving towards your goal with ease.

When you feel ready, snuff out the flame. Leave the orange candle on your altar or set it somewhere safe, as you can relight this each day to help you through change.

Dispose of the white candle in the trash, as this represents the old you that needs to be released.

Taper or Dinner Candles

Taper candles are the tall, thin candles found in candleholders on fancy dining tables. They are slightly wider at the base (about 2 centimetres or ¾ inch) and taper off to a point at the top. They're often around 20 to 24 centimetres (8 to 9½ inches) in height. Tapers burn for about one hour per inch of candle, so these will take longer when used in spell work. I use dinner candles when working seven-day candle spells if I do not have a seven-knob candle. They're excellent to inscribe and anoint or dress with herbs. They also work well for pinned candle spells. Dinner candles are available from a wide variety of stores and online.

+ Best used for homemade seven-knob candles, candle pinning divination, and altar candles

BENEFITS OF TAPER OR DINNER CANDLES

+ Come in a variety of colours
+ Can easily be pinned
+ Can be sectioned into seven-day candles
+ Easy to carve/inscribe
+ Can be dressed with oils and herbs
+ Can be used as a poppet to represent a person

Practice

Pinned Dinner Candle for Decisions

If you need a little help making a decision or choosing between various options, then a pinned dinner candle spell can really help.

You will need

> Blue dinner candle
>
> Candleholder
>
> Four pins, each a different colour to represent the four elements of earth, air, fire, and water
>
> Cup of coffee
>
> Compass
>
> Lighter or matches

Charge your items with the intent to gain clarity and guidance in your decision-making process.

Make yourself a cup of coffee.

Place the candle in its holder, then set that right in front of you.

Pop the compass in front of the candle.

Take the pins and push them into the candle about a third of the way down. Do this one at a time, and space the pins equally around the candle's diameter, as level as you can get them. Each pin represents a cardinal point of the compass:

- North represents the element of earth, practical matters, and home life.
- East represents the element of air, intellect, and intuition.
- South represents the element of fire, passion, creativity, and matters of the heart.
- West represents the element of water, emotions, and dreams.

As you place each pin into the candle, say:

> *With the elements of four*
> *Compass directions, give guidance and more*

Light the wick.

Take a sip of your coffee, then ask your question aloud. State what it is you are trying to make a decision about and ask for guidance.

Sit quietly and watch the flame for any symbols or movement that may help you. Listen carefully for any messages. Slowly sip your coffee as you watch, listen, and wait.

Once the candle wax reaches the pins, watch carefully to see what order the pins fall out in. This will have meaning and can provide insight on your decision. For instance, if the earth pin falls first, then your solution or direction is the most practical or family-orientated one. If the air pin falls first, then your decision should be based on intellect and what seems like the most sensible option. The fire pin falling first could mean you need to follow your heart to make the decision. The water pin falling first might mean you need to listen to your emotions when making the decision. Ultimately, trust your intuition and what the pins represent to you.

Once the pins have fallen, you can snuff the candle out. Dispose of the candle or reuse it for decision-making in the future.

Pillar Candles

Sometimes referred to as *church candles*, pillar candles come in assorted sizes but are tall and wide. The common colour of these is white or cream, but you can find them in various colours. Pillar candles stand on their own and can be dressed in oils and herbs. They can also have different colours of wax dripped onto the top and down the sides for decoration or added spell energy. I like to use these on my altar; I have one dedicated to the God and one to the Goddess. I light them each time I am at my altar in honour of the deities. I also have a large pillar candle that I light each time I do a tarot reading; the candle is dedicated to divination and psychic energy. Pillar candles are easily sourced online or in general stores. Dedicated magical pillar candles are available at occult stores and online.

⁘ Best used for altar and devotional candles

Benefits of Pillar Candles

- Can be found in various colours
- Can be found in scented varieties
- Particularly useful as altar candles
- Can be dressed with oils and herbs
- Easy to carve/inscribe
- Can have images or photographs pinned to them
- Extremely easy to decorate

Practice

Pillar Candle Spell for Gratitude

Everyone has something to be grateful for, and I believe it is a good practice to routinely work a spell of gratitude for Mother Earth and all that she provides for us. Creating and dedicating a pillar candle for this type of spell works really well. You can reuse the same candle each time you perform this spell so that nothing is wasted.

You will need

Brown pillar candle

Candleholder

Lighter or matches

Almond oil

Lemon essential oil

Lavender essential oil

Dried, ground lemon peel

Knife or needle to carve with

Charge your items with the intent of gratitude and thanks.

Using a knife or needle, carve the words *thank you* into the side of the candle, either horizontally or down the side, from top to bottom.

On the other side of the candle, carve a moon symbol (for gratitude) and the symbol for Virgo (to represent harvest and the rewards that you are thankful for).

Add a few drops of lemon and lavender essential oil to your almond oil. Use this blend to dress the candle, dressing towards you to bring gratitude in.

Next, roll the candle in dried, ground lemon peel.

Set the candle in a safe holder. Light the flame and sit quietly for a while, thinking about all that you are grateful for.

When you are ready, say:

> *Mother Earth, I send my thanks to you*
> *Blessings and grateful energy for all you do*

Snuff the candle out and leave it on your altar or in a safe place to be reused next time you repeat the spell.

Rolled Beeswax Candles

Rolled beeswax candles are sheets of beeswax rolled around a central wick to form a candle. They come in assorted sizes and colours. Rolled candles are useful because you can carefully unwrap the wax; pop herbs, spices, or petitions inside the candle; and then reroll them. Rolled beeswax candles and beeswax sheets can be sourced online or at craft stores.

* Best used for spell work

BENEFITS OF ROLLED BEESWAX CANDLES

* Come in a variety of colours
* Burn fairly quickly
* Can be filled with herbs and petitions
* Can be used as a poppet to represent a person

Practice

Rolled Beeswax Candle Spell for Balance

Working with two candles is perfect when you need balance, and rolled beeswax candles are a great choice for this type of magic because they burn quickly and can be filled with herbs to add extra power.

You will need

> 2 blue beeswax candles
>
> Lighter or matches
>
> 2 candleholders
>
> Dried chamomile (use herbs or undo a chamomile tea bag)
>
> Dried honeysuckle flowers
>
> 2 slips of paper
>
> Blue pen
>
> Cauldron or fireproof dish

Charge all the items with your intent.

Mix together a few pinches of dried chamomile and dried honeysuckle.

If you are using beeswax sheets, sprinkle some of the herb mix into each and carefully roll each wax sheet up around a wick. If your candles are ready-made, hold each one in your hand until the wax is slightly warm and very carefully unroll them, sprinkle the herb mix inside each one, and then roll them back up.

Set the candles in the holders.

Take one slip of paper and write down the things that are knocking your life off-balance; it could be your workload, emotions, family life, or something else. Jot down all that you can think of. Fold the slip of paper away from you and place it in front of the first candle.

Take the other slip of paper and write down the things that will bring more balance into your life. Jot down everything that comes to mind. Fold this petition paper towards you to bring the energy in. Set this in front of the second candle.

Light the flame on the first candle and say:

I release and let go that which serves me no good
Unbalanced life and things that I "should"
Let me move forward from unbalance in life
Allow me to leave trouble and strife

Take the petition slip with all the off-balance words written on it and catch it alight using the candle flame, then drop it into the cauldron and allow it to burn out.

Watch the first candle flame as it burns, visualising all that you had on your list disappearing or releasing. Allow the candle to burn out.

Once the first candle has burned out, light the second candle and say:

Power of candle magic and light
Bring me balance and make it right

Take the petition slip with all the things that will bring you balance. Catch it alight from the candle flame, then drop it into the cauldron and allow it to burn out.

Watch the candle flame as it burns. Visualise all that you have written on your list bringing balance and harmony into your life. Allow the candle to burn out.

Container or Jar Candles

Container or jar candles are poured directly into a glass jar or a metal tin. They come in all sizes, shapes, and scents. The larger ones have several wicks. I do not use container candles for spell work, as they usually burn for a long time, but they make good altar or dedication candles. They're available in a wide variety of stores and online.

* Best used for devotional or altar candles

BENEFITS OF CONTAINER OR JAR CANDLES
* Come in a variety of colours
* Come in a variety of scents
* Easy to draw or paint sigils and symbols on
* Images can be stuck to the outside container

Practice

Container Candle Happiness Spell

Working a happiness candle spell can be done on a regular basis. Even lighting it for a couple of minutes each morning works really well because it gives a nice boost of happy, joyful energy. A container candle works well for this since you can just relight the same candle each time.

You will need

> Container candle; go with one that make you smile when you look at it
>
> Lighter or matches

This spell is super easy and only requires a container candle and your visualisation skills.

Charge the container candle with the intent of bringing happy and joyful energy into your life.

Light the wick. Say an affirmation as you light it, something like:

> *Candle magic, flame so bright*
> *Bring me happy and positive energy so light*

Sit for a couple of minutes, allowing happy thoughts to fill your mind. Draw positive energy from the candle into your body and soul.

When you are ready, snuff the candle out. This can be relit whenever you'd like to repeat the spell.

Prayer, Devotional, or Seven-Day Candles

These have various names, but they are tall, cylindrical glass containers with the candle wax poured directly in. They're slightly different from a jar or container candle, as they generally have an image on the outside. The image may be of a deity, saint, tarot image, sigil, or another symbol, such as a veve for Voodoo practitioners.

These large candles typically burn for between sixty and seventy hours. They're sometimes called seven-day candles, with the intention that they are lit for a period of time over the course of seven days whilst working a spell.

This builds momentum for the spell and adds more energy to it each day; the energy is released on the seventh day to work its magic. I tend not to use devotional candles for spell work because they burn for such an extended period of time; for seven-day spells, I use the seven-knob candles.

I prefer to use these candles for devotional purposes. I sometimes put a tarot card behind the candle, a crystal in front, or a circle of herbs around the base as an offering. You can change the "extras" each time you light the candle if you wish. These types of candle can be sourced from occult stores and some online outlets.

+ Particularly useful for altar or devotional use

Benefits of Prayer, Devotional, or Seven-Day Candles
+ Come in a variety of designs

Practice

Prayer Candle Spell

A prayer candle is used for connection to the Divine, deity, or whatever image is displayed on the jar. Use this spell for focus and connection, or for any insight you might be seeking.

You will need
A prayer candle of your choice

Lighter or matches

Set the prayer candle in front of you, light the wick, and focus on the container's image, whatever it might be. If it is a deity, ask any questions you might have, or just send your gratitude to them for watching over you. If the image is a tarot card, focus on the picture and the meaning of the card and what it can bring to you.

Look at the image for as long as you need, then snuff out the flame. The candle can be relit each time you want to spend time focusing on it.

Seven-Knob Candle

The seven-knob candle is a specifically shaped candle that is created from seven wax knobs stacked on top of each other. Each knob can be dressed with oil and herbs or carved with symbols or sigils.

One knob is burned each day for a period of seven days. This is good for building up the energy of a spell. Usually, the candle focuses on one main intent, but different aspects of that intent are worked with each day as energy accumulates. The candle's full power is released on the seventh day. You could also use just repeat the same intent each day for seven days. The idea is that the momentum and energy of the spell builds each day until you release it.

You can create your own seven-knob candle by scoring a candle at intervals to separate it into sections. The same effect can be created by placing pins at intervals; burn the candle until the pin drops out, snuff the candle, and then burn to the next pin on the following day. Ready-made seven-knob candles can be found at occult stores and from some online outlets.

- Good for gaining momentum for a spell

BENEFITS OF SEVEN-KNOB CANDLES

- Come in a variety of colours
- Can easily be dressed with oils and herbs
- Symbols or sigils can be carved/inscribed on each knob
- Can be pinned

Practice

Seven-Knob Candle Spell for Self-Care

This spell works well with seven-knob candles, but you could use seven individual spell candles instead. The intent of this spell can easily be modified, but in this example, we will focus on self-care.

You will need

Seven-knob candle

Candleholder

Lighter or matches

Each of the seven knobs on your candle represents a day of the week, a planet, and a general theme:

+ Monday / Moon / Emotion
+ Tuesday / Mars / Activity
+ Wednesday / Mercury / Communication
+ Thursday / Jupiter / Growth
+ Friday / Venus / Love
+ Saturday / Saturn / Structure
+ Sunday / Sun / Energy

These correspondences can help you check in with yourself and figure out where you aren't getting your needs met.

On Monday, light the candle and say:

Light and energy of the moon, I ask of thee
Bring for my emotions, stability

Allow the candle to burn whilst you sit and visualise being in control of your emotions. Once the first knob has been fully burned through, snuff out the candle.

On Tuesday, light the candle and say:

Light and energy of Mars, I ask of thee
A life full of enjoyable activity

Allow the candle to burn whilst you sit and visualise going out and doing things that you enjoy. Once the second knob has been fully burned through, snuff out the candle.

On Wednesday, light the candle and say:

Light and energy of Mercury, I ask of thee
Clear and concise communication ability

Allow the candle to burn whilst you sit and visualise clarity and clear communication between you and others. Once the third knob has been fully burned through, snuff out the candle.

On Thursday, light the candle and say:

Light and energy of Jupiter, I ask of thee
Prosperity, abundance, and personal growth for me

Allow the candle to burn whilst you sit and visualise financial stability and being content with yourself. Once the fourth knob has been fully burned through, snuff out the candle.

On Friday, light the candle and say:

Light and energy of Venus, I ask of thee
Comfort, friendship, and love for my family and me

Allow the candle to burn whilst you sit and visualise being surrounded by good friends and a happy family. Once the fifth knob has been fully burned through, snuff out the candle.

On Saturday, light the candle and say:

Light and energy of Saturn, I ask of thee
Bring order, balance, and structure to my life for me

Allow the candle to burn whilst you sit and visualise your personal and professional life both in tip-top shape. Once the sixth knob has been fully burned through, snuff out the candle.

On Sunday, light the candle and say:

Light and energy of the sun, I ask of thee
Bring passion and fiery energy to me

Allow the candle to burn whilst you sit and visualise your life being full of energy and passion. Let it fully burn down.

Now that you have worked with each section of the candle, spend a few minutes in reflection. Write down what changes you can make in your life to bring about these qualities.

EXTRAS

If you want to increase the layers of magic in your seven-knob candle spell, you could try some of these suggestions:

- Each section of the candle can be dressed with corresponding oils and herbs. (See chapter 6 for suggestions on which herbs and oils to use.) Dress the section of the candle that you will be burning that day before lighting it.
- Set a crystal in front of the candle that represents the energy and magic of that part of the spell. Add a different crystal each day.
- Carve the symbol for the corresponding planet into each section of the candle.

Novena Candles

The Novena or "nine-day" candle is used in some Roman Catholic churches. The candle is lit and burns continuously over a period of nine days and is not extinguished. It is used to send the same prayer, request, or desire to God each day. Although similar in design to prayer candles, these candles burn uninterrupted for nine days straight. These candles are available from online outlets.

- Best used for devotional or altar candles but also for longer spells

BENEFITS OF NOVENA CANDLES

- Some come in jars with images already on them
- Jar Novena candles can have sigils or symbols drawn on the container
- Plain Novena candles can be dressed with oil and herbs
- Plain Novena candles can be carved/inscribed

Practice

Novena Candle Prosperity Spell

A little extra money is always appreciated, and the Novena candle works well for prosperity spells because a sigil can be drawn on the outside of the container, bringing extra power to the spell. Whilst a Novena candle is meant to burn continuously for nine days, that isn't always safe to do at home. If you do have a safe spot to allow a candle to burn uninterrupted, that is excellent; otherwise, you will need to snuff it each day and relight.

You will need

Novena candle in a glass container

Sharpies or glass pens

Piece of paper

Pen

Lighter or matches

Dried basil

Charge your items with the intent of bringing prosperity into your life.

Take the piece of paper and design a sigil (suggestions on how to work with sigils can be found in chapter 8). When you have a design you are happy with, take your Sharpie or glass pen and draw the sigil onto the container.

Next, add a pinch of dried basil to the top of the candle.

Set the candle in front of you and light the wick. Say:

> *Sigil magic, bring prosperity to me*
> *Basil energy, send money to see*
> *Nine days this spell will be cast*
> *Prosperity magic will then be fast*

Spend some time in front of the flame, fixing the image of the sigil in your mind and visualising money coming to you. When you feel ready, snuff the flame out.

The flame will need to be lit and the chant said every day for nine days total. Each day, spend some time visualising your goal whilst watching the flame.

Once the nine days are finished you can dispose of the candle, or use it again at a later date for the same spell.

Shaped Candles

Candles come in a huge array of shapes and figures, frequently depicting people or animals. The magic worked with shaped candles is done via solid imagery and correspondences. When you do spells with shaped candles, make sure the shape/figure matches your intent. The connection should make sense to you; trust your intuition. Shaped candles can be harder to track down, but some occult stores and online outlets do stock them. You may want to keep an eye out at certain times of the year. For example, cat- and skull-shaped candles can often be found in stores during the month of October because of Halloween.

- Useful for specific, directed spell workings

CAT-SHAPED CANDLES

Black cats have been associated with magic and Witchcraft throughout history. This can be dated back to the thirteenth century, when Pope Gregory IX stated black cats were an incarnation of Satan. In medieval Europe, cats were also linked with Witches. It was said that both cats and Witches "[exhibited] a healthy disrespect for authority."[9] It was even suggested that Witches could turn into black cats.

In other cultures, though, cats were honoured and thought to bring prosperity. Because of this, cat candles can be used for luck and money spells. They also work well for shape-shifting spells and, of course, any spell to stick it to authority!

DEVIL-SHAPED CANDLES

A devil-shaped candle can be used for cursing but also to remove negative energy or banish evil spirits. The Devil tarot card represents addiction, so you could use a devil-shaped candle to remove bad habits. "Ol' Horny" is a trickster who enjoys those earthly excesses, so this shape works well with associated magic.

---

9. Elizabeth Yuko, "Why Black Cats Are Associated with Halloween and Bad Luck," History, October 13, 2021, https://www.history.com/news/black-cats-superstitions.

GENITALIA-SHAPED CANDLES

Yup, you can purchase candles shaped like various personal body parts. These candles are used for love and passion spells. They also work well in spells for increasing sexual energy. Names can be carved into each candle.

HUMAN FIGURE CANDLES

These can obviously be used as a poppet to represent the person you are working magic for—or against. Names can be carved into the figure or written on a petition slip and pinned to it. A photograph could be attached to the candle, as could any type of personal item such as fingernails or hair.

LOVERS CANDLES

A candle showing two humans entwined does exactly what it says on the tin: it brings lovers together. The lovers candle is all about passion, romance, and fertility. Names can be carved into each figure on the candle.

PYRAMID CANDLES

The pyramid is all about manifestation and power. I recommend working money and prosperity magic with this shape of candle, but you can use pyramid candles to call in anything that you want, need, or desire.

SKULL-SHAPED CANDLES

A skull candle is great for ancestor work. They are associated with the spirit world and the power of the mind. Skull candles can be dressed with oils and herbs associated with particular spirits or ancestors. Names can also be carved into the candle, or photographs of ancestors can be pinned to it.

Practice

Skull-Shaped Candle Spell for Psychic Abilities

If your psychic abilities need a boost, then working with a skull-shaped candle can really help. Skulls are associated with ancestors and the spirit world, so this shape is perfect for any kind of psychic spell work.

You will need

 Skull-shaped candle, preferably white, black, or purple

 Candleholder

 Lighter or matches

 Star anise

 Knife

 Moonstone tumbled crystal

 Your divination tool of choice

Charge all your items with the intent of increasing your psychic abilities and opening up communication with the spirit world.

Using the knife, scrape a hole into the base of the skull candle and push the star anise into the space.

Set the candle upright on the candleholder.

Place the moonstone crystal in front of the candle.

Light the wick and say:

> *Candle light and psychic energy bright*
> *Shine into the dark and make things light*
> *Psychic skills that need a boost nigh*
> *Bring me communication from on high*

Now take out your divination tool (tarot cards, a pendulum, runes, etc.) and do a reading whilst the skull candle burns. The reading can be about any subject—the purpose of this spell is to boost your psychic abilities to aid your divination skills.

Once your reading is done, snuff out the candle. This can be relit next time your psychic skills need a boost.

Dedicated Zodiac Candles

You can purchase candles that are specifically dedicated to the signs of the zodiac. I have seen them as two-coloured candles and as glass prayer candles. They can be used to represent you or the person you are working magic for via the corresponding zodiac sign. Occult stores and spiritual shops often have these, or they can be found online.

+ Best used as altar candles or for longer spells

BENEFITS OF DEDICATED ZODIAC CANDLES
+ Come ready-made and dedicated to each zodiac sign (or you can create your own by carving zodiac symbols into a candle)
+ Can be dressed with oils and herbs

Practice

Zodiac Candle Healing Spell

Incorporating zodiac signs into your spell work can create a strong connection for you or another person when doing healing magic.

You will need
Zodiac candle to represent the person needing healing; purchase one ready-made, if possible

Candleholder

Lighter or matches

Knife or needle to carve

Olive oil

Dried, ground thyme

6 dried rose petals

3 pieces of selenite

Charge all your items with the intent of healing and good health.

Take the candle and carve the zodiac sign of the person requiring healing onto one side of the candle. (If you bought a ready-made zodiac candle, you can skip this step.)

Next, carve the symbol for Virgo onto the candle to represent healing and health.

Dress the candle with olive oil, dressing it towards you to bring in healing energy. Then, roll the candle in dried, ground thyme.

Set the candle in a safe holder.

Place the rose petals and selenite around the base of the candle so that they form a circle, a ring of healing energy.

Light the wick. Visualise healing energy being sent to the person that requires it. See them growing in energy and strength. Say:

Healing energy and magic made
Strength and health to be regained
Good health and healing sent around
Healing to bring you back abound

When you are ready, snuff out the candle. This candle can be relit for a number of days or until the person is well again.

Scented Candles

Our noses are bombarded with the amount of scented candles now available. I tend to think of scented candles as something to make the room smell nice rather than a magical tool, but you can use them in spell work if you choose. Be mindful of picking a candle that has been scented with natural oils rather than chemical perfumes—once you light the wick, those chemicals are transferred into the air you breathe.

Also remember that some scents are poisonous to pets. Most chemical scents can be toxic, and some essential oils are too, such as cinnamon, pine, pennyroyal, tea tree, and wintergreen. If you have pets, do your research before lighting a scented candle.[10]

+ Best used for altar candles

BENEFITS OF SCENTED CANDLES
+ Come in a variety of sizes
+ Come in a variety of scents

---

10. I recommend visiting www.dogsnaturallymagazine.com.

Practice

Scented Candle Spell to Remove Obstacles

Life puts obstacles in our way sometimes, or we come up against the occasional blockage. Using the magic of scent can help remove whatever is in your way, creating a clear path so you can move forward.

You will need

 Scented candle, preferably coloured white or red; suggested scents are coconut, mint, or bergamot

 Candleholder

 Lighter or matches

 Slip of paper

 Pen

 Cauldron or fireproof dish

 Pinch of dried mint

Charge your items with the intent of removing obstacles that are blocking your path.

Take the slip of paper and write the words "remove all obstacles in my way" onto it. Draw a cross over the top of your words, then sprinkle a pinch of dried mint into the centre of the paper.

Fold this petition away from you to remove negative energy, being careful as you fold so that the herbs are contained inside.

Light the wick of the candle and say:

> *Scent that floats upon the wind*
> *Obstacles in my pathway now rescind*
> *Release the way and let me be free*
> *Reveal a clear journey for me to see*

Take the folded petition and catch it alight on the flame, then drop the paper into the cauldron so it burns out.

For a while, sit and watch the candle's flame. Visualise any obstacles being removed or blockages being released, allowing you to move forward.

When you are ready, snuff out the flame. You can relight this candle each day over the span of five days or until the blockage is removed.

Floating Candles

You may have seen small candles designed to float on the surface of water. (This effect can also be achieved with most tea lights.) Burn time for floating candles will vary depending on the size, but as a guide, five-centimetre (two-inch) floating candles will burn for about four to five hours, and seven-and-a-half-centimetre (three-inch) floating candles for about eight to ten hours. They work well for outside rituals. Float the candles in a bowl of water or in a cylindrical glass vase filled with water. Floating candles can be found at most stores and online.

- Best used for longer spell workings
- They also make lovely seasonal decorations or altar candles

BENEFITS OF FLOATING CANDLES

- Come in a variety of colours
- Come in a variety of scents
- Bring in the element of water

Practice

Floating Candle Spell

Floating candles are wonderful to work magic with, and they're simple to make! These candles can be made for any intent—just add corresponding herbs, spices, and plant matter into the water. For an extra boost, tie in the power of the moon phase by using charged moon water.

You will need

Clean jam/mason jar

Water (tap water, spring water, distilled water, or moon water)

Floating candle or small tea light

Corresponding herbs, spices, and plant matter

Hold the jar in your hands and charge it with your intent.

Collect all the ingredients you'd like to place in the jar. Be mindful that you do not want to overload it or the candle will not have room to float on top. You can use all sorts of things such as spices, leaves, seeds, flower petals, pieces of bark, or twigs. You can even use water-safe crystals. See part 2 for corresponding ingredients or trust your intuition.

Charge each item with your intent before placing it in the jar.

Then, fill the jar up with water, leaving at least a two-and-a-half-centimetre (one-inch) gap at the top.

Carefully float your candle on the surface of the water.

Light the candle and focus on your intent.

NOTE

Moon water is easily made! Fill a jar with water, then place it outside under the moonlight. You could also place the jar inside, on a windowsill; make sure the reflection of the moon can be seen in the surface of the water. Leave the jar out overnight. In the morning, it will be fully charged with the moon's energy. You can create moon water during any phase of the moon, including the dark moon. (Keep in mind that you will not see a moon reflection under the dark moon.)

Hag Torches

Hag torches, hag candles, Witch candles…Different names for the same thing. A hag candle is created with a core of dried mullein and coated with beeswax and various dried flowers and herbs. Mullein has been used throughout history to dispel evil and bring about protection. In ancient Rome, stalks of mullein were dipped in tallow and used as torches carried during funerals.[11] Nowadays, hag torches are used to remove negative energy or evil spirits, and they're also used in baneful magic.

Hag torches are referred to as torches because they are not technically a candle, as they do not have a wick. It is safest to use hag torches outside, as they can flare. They can be used indoors as long as you do so with caution.

---

11. Rebecca Beyer, "The Hag's Taper: Mullein," *Blood and Spicebush* (blog), September 26, 2017, http://www.bloodandspicebush.com/blog/the-hags-taper-mullein.

They are good for cleansing and purifying your environment, sacred space, or ritual area. They can also help you make a connection to the Otherworld.

Hag torches may be a little hard to track down, as they are usually hand-crafted. I have seen them in occult stores. You might be able to find them online.

+ Best used for cleansing and purifying the home

BENEFITS OF HAG TORCHES
+ Can be customised depending on the types of herbs and flowers used

Practice

Cleansing Hag Torch Spell

It is surprising how quickly negative energy can build up in our homes. A candle spell is an alternative to the usual cleansing with smoke. Be mindful that hag torch candles can flare; I like to keep them in one place, because it is safer than wandering around the home. You can also set the hag torch outside in your garden to cleanse the boundaries of your property.

You will need
Hag torch

Lighter or matches

Candleholder

Set your hag torch in a safe holder. You may need to cut the base of the hag torch to be able to set it in a candleholder.

If it is possible, set your candle up in the centre room of your home.

Light your hag torch. You may need to snip off the top so that you get a "wick," which will be part of the mullein stalk.

Sit quietly and watch the flame. Visualise the energy from the candle spreading out into each room of your home, one room at a time. See the energy filling each room and spreading into the corners from floor to ceiling, clearing out any negativity and bringing in positive vibes. (If you prefer, you can get up and carry the torch around as you walk into each room, but since hag torches can flare, it is safer to stay put.)

You may want to say a chant as you visualise, something like:

Hag torch with your flame so bright
Clear out negative energy with all your might
Make my home clear and free
Fill with only positive energy

Hag torches usually take about fifteen minutes to burn out, so sit and visualise until it has finished burning.

Outdoor Bug-Repellent Candles

Candles designed for outdoor use are often encased in glass or tin to protect them from the elements. They are usually scented, sometimes to keep bugs away. These candles are not often used for magic, but they work well if you are holding an outdoor ritual—they can set the mood or provide ambient lighting. These candles are generally available in all kinds of stores.

+ Best used outside for lighting and effect

BENEFITS OF OUTDOOR BUG-REPELLENT CANDLES
+ Good for lighting areas
+ Can keep bugs away

Lighting Tapers

Tapers for lighting are long, slim candles, essentially just a wick with a light coating of wax. Lighting tapers are used to light other candles. These are useful if you have several candles that need to be lit at one time, or if you have a tea light or small candle at the bottom of a glass jar or inside a lantern. Lighting tapers are readily available in all kinds of stores.

+ Extremely useful if you need to light lots of candles or have a tea light at the bottom of a jar

Personal Note

As candle magic is my go-to for any spell work, I keep a stash of candles on hand. I thought it might be useful to share which candles I like to work with, and what I use them for.

My candle of choice is the small spell candle, and I have these in a variety of colours. I have several small pillar candles that I use as dedicated candles for deities and animal guides. I light a large pillar candle when I read tarot. I use tea lights when I create candle and crystal grids, but I tend not to use them for general spell work, as they take too long to burn out. I also keep a few dinner candles handy; I use these to create my own seven-knob candles or add them to sabbat altars. I have a few scented votive candles, but I don't usually work magic with these—they are used around Yule to make the house smell festive!

Candleholders

An obvious subject that is sometimes overlooked is choosing a candleholder. Candleholders come in a variety of materials such as glass, wood, plastic, and metal. You will need one for most—if not all—of your candles. I have worked with several different types, and whilst I love the idea of a wooden candle-holder, I have found that if you are not careful, the candle flame burns the wood when it gets low. I haven't used plastic candleholders, but I suspect they do the same—melted plastic would not be a good addition to your candle spell, your furniture, or the air. Traditional candlestick holders can be sourced in thrift and charity stores inexpensively; some of them are very fancy. I prefer to stick to ceramic candleholders in my spells.

Votives and pillar candles do stand on their own, but you generally need something to set them on so that the melting wax does not end up all over. Votives work well in glass jars or cups. Pillar candles can be stood on coasters, glass or ceramic dishes, or pieces of wood.

Tea lights really do need something to stand on or sit in, as the metal tin gets very hot. There are plenty of tea light holders available to purchase. Some are made from wood or even hollowed-out crystals, but a jam jar works just as well.

Most jars and tins get hot when the candle has been burning for some time. Bear this in mind. If I am using a candle in a jar or tin, I put it on a coaster or set a piece of wood underneath it so that the surface below is not damaged by the heat.

Does it matter what type of holder you use, beyond the practicalities? Candleholder shapes and designs add yet another layer of energy to your spell working. A skull-shaped candleholder is perfect for ancestor magic or spirit work. Love spells could be worked with heart-shaped candleholders. And, of course, there are plenty of candleholders on the market with moon and sun imagery.

I have coloured glass holders that I use to correspond with the four elements: a red one for fire, a blue one for water, a yellow one for air, and a green one for earth. I have a candleholder that is shaped like a bat; it works well to bring in the magical energy of the bat; this applies to all sorts of animal-shaped holders. For the sabbats, I have a set of tea light holders; each one has the name of the sabbat and images that correspond to it. I also have a couple of lovely wrought-iron candleholders that bring in the elements of fire and water. (Bear in mind that these would not be good holders to use if trying to work with the world of the fairy, as they hate iron.)

If you are interested in sourcing your own candleholders, holders for dishes or coasters could be repurposed. Leave a bit of space around the candle so you can add items like crystals or herbs. Chip 'n dip dishes also make excellent candleholders. Set a tea light in the centre "dip" part; other spell ingredients, such as crystals or herbs, can be placed in the "chips" part.

Large, flat stones or offcuts of wood make sturdy surfaces on which to set candles. I have a long piece of oak that was an offcut from our kitchen unit that I work candle spells on. I stand the spell candles directly on the wood, held in place by a few drops of hot wax. I have a large, flat stone I brought home from the seaside that I use in the same way. They both provide a solid, sturdy base, and they incorporate the elements too: the wood brings an earthy energy, and the stone brings not only earth, but the energy of water too.

Get creative with your candleholders. Tall candleholders can have wire, ribbon, or thread wrapped around them (just keep these materials away from where the candle flame will be). Photographs or images can be tied to candleholders too. Images and symbols can be painted on glass and metal candle-holders. Wooden holders can be painted or have symbols carved or burnt into them. You could even glue items to the holder, such as buttons, dried flowers and herbs, or glitter.

All of this is to say, it is useful to think about which candleholder(s) you choose for your spell work. Consider how well it will support the candle and also what, if any, energy it will add to your spell working.

Personal Note

From experience, I recommend "sticking" tall candles in the holder before lighting them, whether you're using a candelabra or a smaller holder. To do this, light a candle (I use an odd candle stub for this rather than the new candle) and drip hot wax into the holder. Then, quickly, while the wax is still warm, push the new candle into its setting. Hold it in place for a few seconds until the wax has set. This stabilises the candle in its holder.

Cost-Effective Candles

If you are working on a strict budget, or if you just want to save a little money, here are some tips to make your candle purchases more cost-effective:

- Buy small spell candles or even taper candles and cut them up. Use a sharp knife to cut each one in half, or even into thirds. Trim the top of each piece so you have a wick to light. You have made yourself two or three candles from one!
- Check dollar/pound stores and charity/thrift shops for candles, as they usually have them for very good prices. Keep an eye on the ingredients, though, as some of the cheaper ones are full of chemicals.
- I often buy candles during sales at particular times of the year. After Halloween, stores might have skull candles; after Yule, they sell sparkly red and green candles at sale prices.
- Supermarkets usually stock a few candles, so keep a look out when doing your grocery shopping too.

CHAPTER FIVE

Methods and Ways

Apart from the actual waxy candle, there are other ways you can add power and energy to your candle magic spells. The methods in this chapter all add an extra oomph to your magic and help move spells along. Just like the layers of an onion, there are layers of a spell, each one building upon the other. Working with extra layers not only adds to a spell's power, it also gives you more focus. These "extras" take more time to work with, but they are definitely worth the effort. If a job is worth doing, it is worth doing properly!

Petition Papers

A petition paper is a representation of your intent in paper form. It is a formal written request. Petition papers carry a word (or several words) that sums up the intent and focus of a spell. You do not need to write an essay on a petition paper—write down a few key power words that represent the intent of your spell. For example, if I was working a spell to bring me courage for a speaking engagement, I might write "Courage and Confidence" on the petition paper. For a spell to release bad habits, I could write "Release and let go my bad habits." If this sounds simple, that's because it is—petition papers don't need to be complicated.

You can write on petition paper with a pencil, pen, paintbrush, quill, or whatever you feel is right. I often write with a coloured felt pen, coordinating the colour with the intent of my magic. You could also use magical inks.

Once you've written a petition paper, what do you do with it? Here are some ways you could integrate a petition paper into your spell work:

- Pin it to your candle or the wick of your lamp.
- Place it underneath your candle.
- Place it in front of the candle.
- Use the candle's flame to set it alight and safely burn it.
- Roll the petition paper inside an unlit beeswax candle, then light that candle as part of your spell.

After your candle spell is done, it is time to dispose of any leftover petition paper. There are many ways to do this, some of which I'll share in a moment, but trust your intuition. Your method may change for each spell working. Remember to think about how and where you dispose of your petition paper: is your method both safe and eco-friendly? Here are some ways you could dispose of your petition paper:

- Drop it into water.
- Leave it out in the sun, the rain, or under the moon.
- Bury it in the earth.
- Roll or fold it, then carry it with you or place it on your altar.
- Tear it up and throw it into the wind.
- Toss it in the trash.
- Flush it down the toilet.

What you choose to do with your petition paper will depend on how you feel about its energy, as well as your personal preferences when doing spell work. If a spell relates to emotions, then a watery ending for its petition would work well. If a spell is about money or material things, then burying the petition paper in soil would bring in the earth element. For anything passionate or creative, setting the paper alight using the candle flame brings in the fire element. If you feel the candle spell did the job perfectly as it is, then throwing the petition paper in the trash is good enough.

To sum it up: writing a petition paper puts the intent out there; working candle magic sets the energy in motion; disposing of the petition paper after the spell wraps everything up nicely.

Type of Paper

What type of paper should you use for a petition paper? It is up to you and may depend on what you have available. There are many options, from the ordinary and easily obtained to the fancy and more complicated. Some of my suggestions are notepaper, business cards, toilet paper, coloured craft paper, or natural items such as leaves. Remember that if you are burning or burying your petition, it needs to be written on a biodegradable material.

My go-to is a slip cut or torn from a sheet of printer paper, mainly because it is easily available to me. If you prefer, you can purchase fancy paper and use it specifically for spell work. You can buy paper in all sorts of thicknesses, finishes, and colours at craft stores; your paper can be customised to correspond to the intent of your spell working.

Name Papers

Similar to a petition paper, a name paper is used in many folk magic practices as a way of connecting the energy of a person to a spell. A slip of paper (usually from a brown paper bag) is torn, not cut with scissors. I like the energy that torn paper carries with it; somehow it seems more magical than a shape cut with scissors. Tearing paper into shape is my preferred method of creating both name papers and petitions.

In the centre of the name paper, write the name of the person the spell is for or directed at. Use their full name if you know it. Business cards work really well as name papers, as they already have the name of the person and a connection to them. You can also use a photograph if you have one; just write the person's name on the back of the image.

Practice

Creating a Name Paper

To work a spell with a name paper, after you have written the name on it, do the following:

1. Pick a word or two that align with your intent, then write the word(s) over the top of the name. If you are working attracting magic, turn the paper clockwise and write the word(s) again. If you are working banishing magic, turn the paper counterclockwise and rewrite the word(s).

2. Starting at one edge of the paper, write a sentence describing your goal. Write in one continuous motion, turning the paper as you write so that the sentence circles the names and words already on the paper.

3. Dress the name paper by adding a dab of an oil blend to each corner.

4. Fold the paper towards you for attracting magic, or away from you for dispelling.

5. The name paper can then be pinned to a candle or set underneath it. It could also be dropped into a jar for a jar spell.

Magical Ink

You can absolutely write your spells and petitions with a pen or pencil, but if you want to add a little something extra, you can use magical ink. Magical inks can be purchased from most good occult stores, but they are also easy to make. The base of magical ink is water. A general rule of thumb is one part water to two parts ingredients (fruits, herbs, bark, etc.).

Bring your mixture to a boil and simmer for twenty to thirty minutes until you get the saturation of colour you want. Strain, then stir in three or four teaspoons of gum arabic powder. (This helps the ink to be less runny and adhere to the paper well.) Once cool, add a teaspoon of alcohol to preserve the ink; vodka works well.

Here are some suggestions for magical ink ingredients:

- Most berries and barks can be made into ink. Hawthorn berries and cinnamon bark in particular work well. Boil them until you get the colour you want; the darker the better, as the ink tends to lighten as it dries.

- Teabags and coffee can be used for a deep brown ink.

- Dragon's blood resin is used to make dragon ink. Grind the resin to a fine powder and then add to water, stirring until the powder dissolves. This can be done with any resin, including frankincense and myrrh.

- Vegetables and fruits such as beetroot and blackberries can be used to create glorious ink colours. Onion skins also work well. Root vegetables need to be boiled, then mashed and sieved. Blackberries can be mashed cold and strained.

- Flower petals and herbs can be boiled and strained.

- A few drops of essential oil can be added for a power boost, and it gives your magical ink a scent.

Practice

Making Magical Red Ink

Red ink in particular is good for love, strength, passion, and creativity spells. Writing your petition in your own magical ink brings extra energy to your spell work and adds a personal connection, as you have made the ink yourself. You can boost that magic even more by adding corresponding essential oils.

You will need

Small saucepan

Sieve/mesh strainer

Chopping board

Knife

1 large beetroot

Small jar with lid

Optional

1 teaspoon vodka (or rubbing alcohol)

Variations

Beetroots carry the magic of grounding, love, and passion, so you could add beetroot essential oil to incorporate those qualities.

To create a grounding ink: Add 6 drops of patchouli essential oil

To create a love ink: Add 6 drops of rose essential oil

To create a passion ink: Add 6 drops of cardamom essential oil

Dice the beetroot into small cubes.

Place the diced beetroot into a saucepan and pour in just enough water to cover the cubes.

Put on the stove on a high heat and bring to a boil, then turn the heat down to medium. Simmer until the beetroot is soft, about twenty minutes.

Strain the liquid from the pan into your jar. Leave the beetroot to cool.

Once the beets are cool enough to handle, take a couple of small pieces and push them through your sieve. Pop the beetroot pulp into the jar with the beetroot water. Stir well and allow to cool to room temperature.

Once the mixture has cooled, stir in the alcohol and/or essential oil, if using.

Practice

Making Magical Psychic Ink

This recipe uses marigold petals to bring a psychic energy to your magical ink, but you can substitute the marigold petals for any flower petal or herb.

You will need

Small saucepan

Sieve/mesh strainer

Glass jar with lid

Gum arabic

1 cup (236 mL) of water

2 cups (or big handfuls) of marigold petals

Optional

Marigolds carry the magical property of psychic energy; you can boost this by adding 3 drops of cinnamon essential oil.

Place the marigold petals and water into the saucepan and bring to a boil over a high heat. Once the mixture is boiling, reduce the heat to medium and allow it to simmer for about half an hour.

Strain the liquid into your jar.

Stir in four teaspoons of gum arabic (and essential oil, if using). Allow to cool to room temperature.

Carving and Inscribing

If you want to add more intent to your candle, you could carve runes, numbers, letters, words, symbols, or sigils into it. Use a toothpick or a small knife to carve your design into the candle wax. I use a tattoo needle to carve my candles; the needle was used during a ritual tattoo, and the artist kindly gave me the needle afterwards. Not only does it have a sharp tip for carving into the candle, but it also carries my own blood magic.

Any wording can be carved into a candle. You can write in a straight line along the side of the candle, from wick to base, for things you wish to release, or you can write up the side of the candle, from base to wick, to bring things to you. Words and designs could also be carved in a spiral from top to bottom or bottom to top.

There are some who believe that whatever you carve into a candle should be done in one fluid movement—without lifting your knife or pin from the wax until you are finished—the idea being that it helps you focus your energy. The idea is sound but not always practical, particularly if your image is quite detailed. Trust your intuition on this one.

Once the wax is carved, you can go over the carving with a Sharpie or glitter pen to highlight the image if you wish. You could even follow the carving with a glue pen and then add crushed herbs or glitter.

Pinning Your Candle

Pinning a candle means placing a pin into a candle at the spot where the magic will be released. Pinning of the candle is done before you start a spell. Once the candle is lit, you will need to hold your focus and intent on the candle until it melts down enough that the pin falls out. Once the candle releases the pin, the spell is done. This can take some time, which also means it can take a great deal of energy. I tend to put a pin in the top third of a candle for this reason.

Pins can also be used to section a candle. You can create a seven- or nine-day candle by pushing pins down the candle at regularly spaced intervals. If you want to bring a bit of colour magic into the spell, you can use coloured pins. If you don't have pins on hand, you can use a simple, straight dressmaking pin; small hat pins also work quite well. If you have long enough plant thorns, these can be used to pin too; the thorns of a blackthorn are a good option.

Pins have also been used in candle magic for the purposes of divination. Two or more pins are placed into the top section of the candle. A question is asked and the wick is lit. Once the pins fall, the way they land is read as an answer to the query. (We will discuss this in more detail in chapter 16.) Cecil Williamson recorded how a wise woman (Mary Sale from Taunton, England) would pierce a coloured candle with pins. The colour of both corresponded to the type of query she was working with. The candle was then placed in a wooden candlestick set on a round table covered with a cloth. The direction that the pins fell and their distance from the candlestick were used to give a reading.[12]

Sealing the Deal

Sealing documents and letters dates far back in history. Originally, seals were used as a means to verify the authenticity of a document rather than to seal the contents inside. But it sure helped prevent the person delivering the communication from peeking inside!

The ancient Sumerians, Egyptians, and Greeks sealed their communications with clay symbols. In ancient Rome, bitumen was used at first. Then they moved on to beeswax, the use of which then spread across Europe. During the Middle Ages, beeswax was the seal of choice because it was easy to use and took the image of a seal well. But also, bees were believed to be sacred to God, which meant their wax was pure.

---

12. Cecil Williamson, "17 – Candlestick + Candle," Museum of Witchcraft and Magic, accessed April 13, 2023, https://museumofwitchcraftandmagic.co.uk/object/candlestick-candle/.

The use of "sealing wax" is believed to have originated in Europe during the sixteenth century—although most did not contain any wax. The usual colour for sealing wax was red or black, but by the nineteenth century, green was also used. Some sealing waxes also had essential oils added to them.[13]

I love the use of sealing wax; it makes letters seem special, so it makes sense to me to use it in magic too. Wax can "seal the deal" for spell work. I use candle wax in spell work in a number of ways:

* When I create a witch bottle (basically a spell in a jar), I like to seal the lid by dripping wax on top. Not only does it seal in all the ingredients, it also finalises the spell. Oh, and it makes the bottle look really Witchy!

* You can use wax on your petition papers once you have written them. Drip hot wax on top of the words, covering them; I like to do this to seal the words of the spell and my intent. You could sprinkle corresponding herbs on top of your petition words and seal them on the paper with wax too.

* When working with an envelope or folded paper filled with spell ingredients, you can drip wax on the folds to seal everything together.

Wax Charms and Talismans

If you have worked a spell and have some wax leftover, you can dispose of it as discussed in chapter 3, or you can create an ongoing spell charm with it. Small pieces of wax can be warmed in your hands and crafted into charms to carry with you or place on your altar. Small pieces of wax can also be used in witch bottles, fastened to poppets, or added to spell pouches that have the same intent the wax's original candle spell had.

Wax from a protection spell can be sprinkled around the boundary of your home, or pieces can be buried in soil (ideally near your gate or the front of your lot) or put under your doormat. Small pieces of the wax remnants can also be dropped into spell pouches or witch bottles for protection.

---

13. Kathryn Kane, "Sealing…Wax?" *The Regency Redingote* (blog), November 16, 2012, https:// regencyredingote.wordpress.com.

Wax from prosperity and money spells can be rolled into a small disc. Place the disc in your purse to keep money coming in or drop it into spell pouches.

The only wax pieces I do not recommend keeping are those that were used in banishing, releasing, or removing spells.

Charms and talismans can be created from new, unused wax as well. You can pour melted wax into small chocolate or cookie moulds. Crystal chips, spices, plant matter, and herbs can be added whilst the wax is still warm. Allow the wax to set, then push the hardened charms out of their moulds. They can be placed on your altar, carried with you, or used in spell work.

Practice

Protection Wax Charm

Make yourself a wax charm to carry with you! Use wax leftover from a protection candle spell or use a brand-new candle.

You will need

> Black candle (remnants of a protection spell *or* a new spell candle)
>
> 6 black peppercorns
>
> Knife
>
> Small mould or empty tea light tin
>
> Lighter or matches

Charge your items with the intent to bring in protection for you.

Pop the black peppercorns into the base of your mould.

Light the wick of the candle and hold it so that the candle wax drips into the mould. Keep going until all the peppercorns have been covered and there is enough wax to create a decently sized charm. (Ideally, it would fit in the palm of your hand.)

Extinguish the candle. Allow the wax to cool.

Once the wax has set, take the knife and carve the rune symbol Algiz into the surface of the wax.

Carefully push the wax out of the mould. Pop the charm into your pocket, purse, or bag; if you want to help preserve it, place it in a fabric pouch first.

Candle Grids

You can amplify the power of your candle magic by creating a candle grid. You may be familiar with crystal grids; I use candle grids in the same way. I also mix the two. To make a candle grid, all you need is a set of candles and any other items you'd like, such as crystals, herbs, or tarot cards. Tea lights work well for grids, but any type of candle can be used.

Practice

Create a Candle Grid

1. Start with a nice flat, safe space.

2. Set one candle down as your central point, then lay out other candles in a design, a bit like a mandala. The design can be a familiar shape, such as a spiral, star, or pentagram, or you can work with your intuition and make a freeform pattern. Charge each candle with your intent as you place it into your design.

3. Once the grid pattern is set out with candles, add in crystals, tarot cards, or herbs that correspond with your intent to boost the magic. Use your intuition to place these items amongst the candle grid design.

4. Once your design is all laid out, state your intent aloud, then light the central candle. Continue lighting the candles, working outwards. You can light each candle individually, or you can light each candle using the flame of the one before. As you light the wicks, tell the candles what you need from them. You may like to say a chant or play music in the background as you work.

5. Once all the candles are lit, your candle grid magic has been activated. Spend some time sitting quietly, watching the flames and visualising your goal. You may want to meditate as well.

6. Once you feel the spell is finished, snuff the candles or allow them to burn out fully. Cleanse the crystals and tarot cards. Throw away the herbs and any candle remnants.

Candle Poppets

Working with candles as poppets can be extremely successful. Instead of making a fabric, twig, or twine poppet, you can just use a candle. Spell candles or dinner candles work best.

If you are feeling creative and have some spare candle wax, you can melt the wax and create a poppet shape by moulding the wax with your hands once it is cool enough to handle, but still pliable. Figure-shaped candles also work well as poppets since they are already poppet shaped! The idea of a poppet being human shaped is that the poppet represents a person, whether it is yourself or another.

You can also create a poppet with a new candle. The shape of the candle represents the body. To create arms, you could tie pipe cleaners or twine around the candle. Pins can be used to make eyes (or even arms as well). To make a face, you can draw on the candle with a pen. Alternatively, a photograph of the person the poppet is intended to represent can be pinned to or tied around the candle. If you'd like, you can pin a petition to the poppet. Once you're finished moulding your poppet, charge the whole thing with your intent. What you do next is up to you; poppets can be placed on your altar to let the magic work, or you can burn a poppet to release the energy.

A wax poppet can be burned by throwing it into a fire—if you only used decorative items on it that will burn easily and safely. If you didn't add too many extras to the candle, it can be burnt as you would a regular candle. When the spell is finished, dispose of the poppet remnants away from your property. Toss it in a public trash can or bury it (if the items are biodegradable).

Practice

Wax Poppet Binding Spell

Binding spells are useful when you find yourself in a situation where someone is causing you grief but you don't want to work with banishing or cursing. A binding spell stops the person from causing harm to you but does not inflict any physical injury to them.

You will need

Spell candle in burgundy or black

Sesame oil

Dragon's blood essential oil

Piece of brown paper, torn at the edges

Black pen

Twine

Thorn or pin

Firepit or bonfire

Your firepit or bonfire can be lit before you begin creating the poppet, or it can be lit afterwards—whichever is convenient.

Charge the items with the intent of binding a person to bring protection for you or your family.

Add a few drops of dragon's blood essential oil to the sesame oil and dress the candle, working in a clockwise spiral around the candle.

Write the name of the person you wish to stop on the slip of brown paper. Now cross out the name with your pen.

Pin the name paper to the candle with a pin or a thorn.

Take the twine and begin to bind it around the candle in a clockwise motion. Visualise the person causing harm being prevented from doing so and staying out of your way. As you work, say:

Energy of dragon and the powers that be
Bind this person and protect me
Stop them from causing harm so bad
Bind their energy to stop the sad

Tie the twine off in a knot.

Then throw the whole candle into the flames and say:

Flames now burn to seal the spell
Binding is done and all is well
No harm done, but safe and sound
Protection for me is now bound

Merging Candles

I love to do spell work with several candles together. If you place them right next to each other, they burn and melt together, making interesting flame patterns and wax drips and pools. This also helps merge the candles' magical intent. For this method, I have found that smaller spell candles or beeswax candles work best.

As they burn, merging candles combine their intent. For example, I could light a green candle for prosperity, an orange candle for success, and a red candle for power. As they burn, the candles' energies mix; these three colours make an excellent candle magic spell for a new project or venture. I might even get an interesting reading if the different colours of melted wax pool together.

Practice

Clarity, Insight, and Truth Merging Candle Spell

When I need to get to the bottom of a situation, I like to use a merging candle spell because it brings together several intents for a similar goal. In this case, the spell will give you clarity on an issue, showing you the truth, and will provide insight on how to resolve or deal with it.

You will need

> 3 spell candles (or rolled beeswax candles) in different colours: 1 blue, 1 black, 1 white
>
> Lighter or matches
>
> Clove oil mixed with sunflower base oil
>
> Pinch of ground coffee
>
> 3 cloves
>
> High Priestess tarot card
>
> Dish to stand the candles in; I like to use a mirror to provide reflection

Work this spell on a dark moon, on a Monday if possible.

Set your ingredients in front of you. Charge them all with your intent.

Once charged, it is time to dress the candles with the oil blend. Start with the black candle. Dress the candle away from you to uncover the truth.

Next, dress the white candle towards you to bring clarity.

Lastly, dress the blue candle towards you to bring insight.

Stand all three candles next to each other, close enough that they are touching. To set the candles firmly in place, you may have to drip a bit of hot wax (from another candle) onto the dish and stand the candles in it.

Place the High Priestess card behind the candles.

Take a pinch of coffee and sprinkle it over the top of the three candles, saying:

Coffee power, give this spell a boost
Find for me the ultimate truth

Place a clove in front of each candle and say:

Magical power of clove, bring to me
The benefit of insight, truth, and clarity

Light the black candle and say:

Black candle, shine and show to me the truth

Light the white candle and say:

White candle, shine and show to me pure clarity

Light the blue candle and say:

Blue candle, shine and bring to me the gift of insight

Sit quietly and watch the candles as the flames merge and the waxes melt together. See the situation you want resolved in your mind's eye. Look out for any messages in the movement of the flames and listen for any words that might pop into your head.

Allow the candles to burn out completely. If there is a wax puddle afterwards, note any images or shapes you can see that might shed some light on your situation.

Throw any remnants into the trash.

Passing the Flame

Candle magic can be used to "pass the flame." What I mean by this is that magic from one candle flame can be passed on to another candle. An example of this is a candle I have on my altar that carries the energy of the goddess Brighid and the blessings of the Dalai Lama. I attended a festival several years ago that had a central candle. That candle had been lit from an eternal flame in Brighid's temple, which had also been blessed by the Dalai Lama. The candle carried the flame's original energy, and that energy was passed on to all the candles that were subsequently lit from it.

I often pass the flame with my own candles, particularly a friendship one I have. The central candle was dedicated to my inner circle of friends, and candles were lit from it and then passed to my friends so they could have a friendship candle of their own, imbued with our group energy. This can also be done with altar candles dedicated to deity. Light a new candle from the original one and you have passed the energy on.

Practice

Friendship Candle Spell

This spell was designed during a time my inner circle and I were separated for a while and were not able to physically meet up. It can be used for friends, Coven members, and family members to keep your connection strong.

You will need

    Central candle

    1 candle for each person in the group

    1 small tumbled rose quartz for each person

    Lighter or matches

    Heatsafe plate large enough for all the candles to stand on

Hold the central candle in both hands and charge it with the energy of friendship, love, and harmony. Visualise yourself and each member of the group together, happy and content.

Set the central candle in the centre of the plate. Light the wick.

Take each of the other candles in turn and light the wick from the central candle's flame. Place the newly lit candles on the plate, making a circle around the central candle.

When all the candles are lit, pass each tumbled stone over the central candle flame, holding the stone at a safe distance above the flame. Then place each stone in front of a candle.

Say:

> *Friendship, community, and blessings from above*
> *These candles represent our group filled with love*
> *Lit from the central candle flame*
> *Our energy stays connected time and again*
> *Distance may come between all of us*
> *But candle magic brings us together, no fuss*

Snuff out each of the individual candles, leaving the centre one burning.

Carefully wrap together one friendship candle and one of the stones. Do this until all the candles and stones have paired up, then send to each person along with a copy of the blessing. Now each person will have their own candle and stone that are connected to the central group candle and to each other.

Personal Notes

- I used a beautiful twisted, ornate pillar candle as my central candle. I felt it needed to be something special to hold us all together.

- Rose quartz was chosen because it represents love and friendship, but you could use any crystal you are drawn to. You could even use pebbles or shells.

- For the individual candles, I chose dinner/taper candles, using different colours to represent each person.

PART II
AMPLIFYING YOUR MAGIC

CHAPTER SIX

Sensory Magic

In this section you will find corresponding suggestions to add to your candle magic that help boost magical energy. Correspondences play an important part in any kind of spell work. Colour is a good starting point. Colour impacts our thoughts, feelings, and emotions, and it ties in nicely with intent when working a spell. I also share correspondences for herbs and spices. I couldn't work magic without them—they add such an important energy to all of my spells, bringing the magic of Mother Nature with them. The spirit or energy within plant matter really brings something special to spell work.

Do keep in mind that these correspondences are a guide. This is what works for me, but you may feel differently. Trust your intuition. If you don't have something on hand, consider what you do have that could be a good substitute. There are no rules.

Colour Magic

If you want to add power to your candle spell, use a coloured candle that mirrors your objective. The use of colour can change our mood and provoke emotion. Colour has its own vibrations, just as sound does. Using colour in magic helps you tune in to the vibrations of your magical intent. Colour magic could be choosing a specific candle, or it could be extended to include a coloured candleholder, altar cloth, or decorative item.

Traditionally, colours are associated with particular intents, such as black for death and red for love. (These are generalisations.) In this section, I will share some of the correspondences I have with colours, but this is very personal work. How does a colour make *you* feel?

White

A basic white candle covers pretty much every intent. If you cannot decide what colour to work with, white is a useful all-purpose colour.

INTENTS

All purpose, angels, beginnings, blessings, clarity, cleansing, consecration, focus, grace, harmony, hope, initiation, innocence, insight, modesty, moon magic, personal strength, protection, purification, purity, sincerity, truth, unity

Black

Black is not a negative or evil colour. In fact, it can be used for any spell, just as white candles can, because it is a neutral colour.

INTENTS

Absorbing negative energy, banishing, breaking hexes, caution, closure, control, curses, death and rebirth, dispelling negative energy, earth magic, harsh justice, hexing, initiation, negative energy, Otherworld magic, protection, releasing, responsibility, spirit work, stability, strength, truth

Grey

Grey is an "in-between" colour, as it is a mix of white and black. In this way, it becomes a neutral colour. Grey candles can be used in place of silver or brown and have comparable properties.

INTENTS

Age, depression, divination, invisibility, maturity, mourning, reversing spells, stalemates

Brown

A must when working with home or family magic, brown has a strong grounding energy. Like green, it is associated with the element of earth and the direction of north.

INTENTS

Abundance, ancestors, balance, boredom, confidence, the conscious mind, earth magic, endurance, fertility, finances, foundation, grounding, house and home, material needs, nature, protection, resources, sadness, security, stability, tenacity

Pink

Pink is a mixture of red and white. It has a gentler energy, linked more with romance and friendship than red.

INTENTS

Beauty, emotion, emotional relationships, faith, feminine energy, friendship, goddess energy, happiness, harmony, health, hope, kindness, love, morality, revival, romance, self-love, unity

Red

Often seen as the colour of love, red is the most passionate type of love, linked to sex and hot blood! Red is also the colour of the element of fire and the direction of south.

INTENTS

Anger, binding, birth, blood magic, bravery, courage, creativity, desire, energy, enthusiasm, focus, health, life, love, motivation, overcoming, passion, protection, revenge, sexuality, sex magic, stimulation, strength, triumph, victory, vigour, vitality, will

Burgundy

A dark red colour, burgundy brings a very domineering energy with it.

INTENTS

Binding, cursing, domination, persuasion

Orange

Orange is my colour of choice for any kind of success magic. I often pair it with green for money spells. It has a loud confidence and a positive kind of vibe.

INTENTS

Adjustment, ambition, attraction, concentration, courage, creativity, energy, fun, joy, motivation, nurturing, positive energy, prosperity, self-confidence, self-worth, stamina, success, vitality

Yellow

A bright, sunshiny colour that brings happy energy with it, yellow is also the colour of the element of air and the direction of east.

INTENTS

Assurance, awards, charm, clarity, communication, concentration, confidence, creativity, divination, glamour spells, goals, happiness, inspiration, intellect, inventiveness, jealousy, joy, knowledge, luck, positive energy, power, recognition, social skills, solar magic, strength

Green

The colour of money and my preferred colour for prosperity spells, green is also the colour of nature, so it brings fertility energy as well. Green is the colour used to represent the element of earth and the direction of north.

INTENTS

Abundance, balance, beginnings, cowardice, discord, envy, fate, fertility, fortune, growth, healing, health, immortality, inspiration, jealousy, life, luck, maturity, money, nature, prosperity, revitalisation, spring, stability, suspicion, wealth, youth

Blue

Blue represents the element of water and the direction of west. Blue has a deeply healing energy and also has connections to the spirit realm.

INTENTS

Apathy, balance, beginnings, calm, clarity, communication, contemplation, depression, devotion, dreams, emotion, endurance, fidelity, forgiveness, harmony, healing, hope, innovation, inspiration, instinct, intuition, legal affairs, meditation, peace, psychic energy, psychic skills, relaxation, sadness, spirituality, spirit work, spiritual protection, transformation, travel, truth, understanding, water magic

Purple

Purple is the colour I associate with spirituality and the Divine.

INTENTS

Angels, authority, divination, the Divine, goals, inspiration, intuition, loyalty, luxury, meditation, personal power, prosperity, psychic abilities, riches, spirituality, spirit work, success, tranquillity, wealth, wisdom

Violet

Although similar to the colour purple, violet has more blue to it and is less saturated than purple. Violet does have a use in candle magic separate from purple.

INTENTS

Advancing, balance, divination, dreams, finding things, inspiration, intuition, progress

Gold

Gold has a solar energy and strong connections to abundance.

INTENTS

Abundance, celebration, fire magic, God energy, luck, masculine energy, mental power, money, originality, personal skills, prosperity, sun magic, victory, wealth

Silver

Silver brings balance to gold and has a strong lunar energy.

INTENTS

Dreams, feminine energy, goddess magic, intuition, imagination, moon magic, protection, spirit work

Spirit of the Ingredient

No matter what spell ingredient you are working with—whether it is an essential oil, herb, spice, or plant—it has an energy. This energy remains the same whether the ingredient is fresh or dried. Every crystal has an energy and spirit as well. Connecting with the spirit of an ingredient is important because it helps you determine what kind of magic the ingredient can help with and if it is a good fit for your particular spell.

To connect to the spirit of an ingredient, hold the ingredient in your hand. (It can be in a container if needed.) Open your mind and ask the ingredient what it can help you with. Listen for any words or thoughts that pop into your head. Pay attention to any feelings or emotions that rise up. Then, write down what kinds of magic the ingredient is well-suited for; in doing so, you are beginning your own record of correspondences. There are no right answers here. Trust your connection to the spirit of each ingredient.

Knowing the spirit of the ingredient is important, as is knowing its correspondences. Each ingredient will correspond to one of the four elements: earth, air, fire, or water. Most of them are also ruled by a planet. I have included these correspondences in this chapter. Correspondences can be especially useful when creating blends to use in spell work.

Oils

There are a dizzying amount of oils and scents available. Where to even begin? Personally, I like to add essential oils to unscented candles rather than buying scented candles. If I am burning a candle and sending the scent into the air I am breathing, I want it to be natural, not full of chemicals.

Often, I work with a single essential oil. I use a small brush to apply it to a candle, as essential oils can irritate the skin. If you prefer to use your hands to add ingredients to your candle, first mix the essential oil with a carrier/base oil, such as olive or almond. (Base oils—even the olive oil you might have in your kitchen cupboard—can also be used on their own to anoint a candle.)

I must say, using your hands does help you get more of a "feel" for the magic, strengthening your connection to the spell. It does get messy, though!

A mix of essential oils can also be used. In fact, the act of creating an oil blend can add to the magical ritual of a spell. It means you have taken time to think about the different scents and how they work together. You also add your intent to the mixture as you create it. To create your own blend, use your senses. Intuitively feel which essential oils would work well together. If you need to double-check, use a pendulum and ask whether a particular item is right or not. Then, add a few drops of each essential oil to a piece of kitchen towel to see what they smell like together. Mixing essential oils with a base oil without testing it first can be a waste.

As a general rule of thumb, when creating a blend, I use ten millilitres of base oil for every twenty to twenty-five drops of essential oil. I also prefer to work with no more than four or five different essential oils in a blend. In fact, I generally like to stick to three. For one thing, three is a magical number. But also, the more scents you add, the more complicated it all gets. I feel that the energies start to get confused the more ingredients you add.

If oil blends are new to you, then start with the basics. I have included some suggestions for everyday essential oils in the Herbs and Spices section; these would be a good starting point. Some essential oils are really exotic, but that can mean expensive. Once you get the hang of working with oils (or once the joy of creating blends takes hold of you!), you can branch out and add to your collection.

If you're not a fan of essential oils, your magic can still be successful. Sometimes just a simple candle is enough, though I prefer to dress it with base oil at least. The act of dressing a candle is a form of preparation, readying the candle for magical work.

Be Cautious

Essential oils are incredibly potent. They should only be used on the skin if they have been diluted with a base oil first. I also advise blending with a base oil before dressing candles and other magical tools, as the mixture will come into contact with your skin. If you want to add essential oils to an oil burner, bath, or diffuser, you can create a blend without using a base oil. A little goes a long way! As a general rule of thumb, I use ten millilitres of base oil for every twenty to twenty-five drops of essential oil.

Once you've made an essential oil blend, please test a drop or two on a small area of your skin before you go slapping on loads of oil, just in case you are allergic to it. Also, please do take the time to source pure essential oils. There are some on the market that have been watered down or have nasty chemicals added.

Base Oils

There are a number of different base oils on the market, some more accessible (and cheaper) than others. Here is a list of the basic carrier oils that I use and their magical properties.

ALMOND

Magical Properties: Intuition, love, passion, prosperity, psychic powers, lost treasure

Ruled By: Mercury

Element: Air

Energy: Masculine

COCONUT

Magical Properties: Chastity, protection, purification

Ruled By: The moon

Element: Water

Energy: Feminine

OLIVE

Magical Properties: Fertility, healing, integrity, luck, passion, peace, protection, spirituality

Ruled By: The sun

Elements: Fire and air

Energy: Masculine

SESAME

> **Magical Properties:** Energy, prosperity, protection, secrets, strength
>
> **Ruled By:** The sun
>
> **Elements:** Fire and earth
>
> **Energy:** Masculine

SUNFLOWER

> **Magical Properties:** Confidence, courage, fertility, happiness, prosperity, strength, sun magic
>
> **Ruled By:** The sun
>
> **Element:** Fire
>
> **Energy:** Masculine

Infused Oils

A straightforward way to make an oil for magical use is to infuse herb or plant matter in a carrier oil. This is often cheaper than purchasing essential oils, and an infused oil is very easy to make. Some plants make better infusions than others, and some base oils are more stable than others—it is often a case of trial and error. Make sure your plant matter is clean and dry before use. As for your base oil, olive oil is an excellent choice, and sunflower oil also works well.

Practice

Infused Oil Solar Method

1. Fill a dry, clean jar with the flowers, herbs, or leaves of your choice. Leave about 5 centimetres (2 inches) of space at the top.

2. Pour in your oil of choice, fully covering all the plant matter.

3. Place a lid on the top and shake the jar.

4. Place the jar on a warm, sunny windowsill. Shake once a day for about three weeks.

5. After three weeks have passed, strain the herbs out. Pour the infused oil into a clean jar or bottle.

6. Label and store in a cool, dark place. In ideal conditions, an infused oil can last for up to a year.

Practice

Infused Oil Heat Method

If you want a quicker method, you will need a Crock-Pot or double boiler.

1. Place your leaves or flowers inside a Crock-Pot or double boiler. Cover them fully with your oil of choice. Make sure there are at least two-and-a-half centimetres (one inch) of oil above the plant matter.

2. Leave over a very low heat (about 37°C/100°F) for about five hours. At that point, check if the oil has taken the colour and scent of the herbs. If not, leave the mixture heating for a few more hours.

3. Once the oil is the colour and scent of the herbs, turn off the heat and allow the mixture to cool.

4. Strain the herbs out, pouring the infused oil into a clean jar or bottle.

5. Label and store in a cool, dark place for up to six months.

Herbs and Spices

Rolling your candle in herbs and spices can add another layer of power to your spell work. You can also sprinkle herbs and spices around the base of a candle, or on top, if working with a pillar candle. Fresh flowers and leaves can be used to decorate your altar, but when grinding ingredients to roll candles in or to press into wax, dried works better.

In candle magic, you can use just one herb or one spice; basil, perhaps, for a money spell, or cinnamon for a success spell. Creating your own blend using two or three can be very satisfying, though. They do not need to be fancy, exotic herbs and spices either. In fact, I prefer to use items from my own kitchen cupboard! Every plant has a magical energy to it, so each one can be used for spell work, from a humble blade of grass to spices from the East.

I do not work with any spells that require eighty-seven different ingredients; it just becomes too complicated. I prefer to stick to ingredients that are easily obtainable. I would not order an exotic root that costs a fortune and needs to be shipped from the other side of the world, not only because of the costs involved with shipping and the delivery's ecological footprint, but also because it would not be personal to me. Whenever possible, I use herbs and plants that are native to my region. If I can pick them from my own garden, forage in my local area, or purchase them in a local shop, then I am happy. When I seek out an herb or plant personally, this adds a bit more energy to my spell work. But sometimes this is just not possible. No matter how hard I might try, I will never be able to grow a tree in my garden that I can harvest cinnamon from. Instead, I purchase cinnamon from a local shop.

International stores are excellent sources for the ingredients I cannot grow. They sell spices, in particular, at decent prices. Farmer's markets are useful sources for fresh herbs, fruits, and vegetables for spell work too. Not all of my spell ingredients are locally sourced, but I do what I can to help the environment, local traders, and, of course, my pocket.

The number of plants, herbs, spices, and flowers that can be used in magic is huge. In this section, I have shared a list of my most-used ingredients, their correspondences, and suggestions for how to use them.

Basil (Ocimum basilicum)

Magical Properties: Exorcism, happiness, money, peace, prosperity, protection, wealth

Ruled By: Mars

Zodiac Sign: Scorpio

Element: Fire

Energy: Masculine

Usage: Use dried or fresh leaves or as an essential oil

Bay (Laurus nobilis)

Magical Properties: Creativity, healing, power, protection, psychic powers, purification, spirituality, strength

Ruled By: The sun

Zodiac Signs: Aries and Leo

Element: Fire

Energy: Masculine

Usage: Use dried or fresh leaves (whole, crushed, or ground, and they burn well) or as an essential oil

Benzoin (Styrax benzoin)

Magical Properties: Calming, confidence, love, lust, prosperity, purification

Ruled By: The sun and Venus

Zodiac Sign: Capricorn

Element: Air

Energy: Masculine

Usage: Resin can be ground to a powder or in essential oil

Bergamot Orange (Citrus bergamia)

Magical Properties: Banishing, money, purification, success, sun magic, uplifting

Ruled By: Mercury and the sun

Zodiac Signs: Virgo and Aquarius

Element: Air

Energy: Masculine

Usage: Use fresh or dried leaves and flowers, or dried fruit; more commonly found as an essential oil

Black Pepper (Piper nigrum)

Magical Properties: Confidence, exorcism, gossip, jealousy, negativity, protection, strength

Ruled By: Mars

Element: Fire

Energy: Masculine

Usage: Use whole or ground peppercorns or as an essential oil

Blackthorn (Prunus spinosa)

Magical Properties: Divination, exorcism, healing, protection

Ruled By: Saturn and Mars

Zodiac Sign: Scorpio

Element: Fire

Energy: Masculine

Usage: Use fresh or dried flowers, leaves, or bark; the thorns work well in magic too

Cardamom (Elettaria cardamomum)

Magical Properties: Clarity, love, passion, protection, uplifting

Ruled By: Venus and Mars

Element: Water

Energy: Feminine

Usage: Use the seed pods or as an essential oil

Cedar (Cedrus spp.)

Magical Properties: Goddess magic, money, purification, protection

Ruled By: The sun and Jupiter

Zodiac Sign: Sagittarius

Element: Fire

Energy: Masculine

Usage: Use fresh or dried leaves, seed cones, or bark, or as an essential oil, usually made from a variety of cedar and juniper trees and called "cedarwood" oil

Chamomile (Chameamelum nobile, Anthemis nobilis)

Magical Properties: Balance, calming, dreams, love, money, purification, relaxation, sleep

Ruled By: The sun

Zodiac Sign: Leo

Element: Water

Energy: Masculine

Usage: Use the flowers and leaves fresh or dried, or as an essential oil

Chocolate and Cocoa (Theobroma cacao)

Magical Properties: Happiness, love, positive energy, prosperity

Ruled By: Mars

Element: Fire

Energy: Feminine

Usage: I often use squares from chocolate bars as offerings or place them symbolically in front of a candle; cocoa powder or ground cocoa nibs work well for dressing a candle

Chillies (Capsicum spp.)

Magical Properties: Creativity, energy, hex breaking, passion, power, protection

Ruled By: Mars

Element: Fire

Energy: Masculine

Usage: Used dried or fresh chillies or chilli seeds; chilli oil can be easily made by steeping chillies and/or chilli seeds in a base oil such as olive or sunflower

Cinnamon (Cinnamomum zeylanicum, Cinnamomum verum)

Magical Properties: Change, focus, healing, love, lust, power, protection, psychic powers, spirituality, success

Ruled By: The sun

Zodiac Sign: Aries

Element: Fire

Energy: Masculine

Usage: There are two main types of cinnamon: Ceylon cinnamon is the sticks and ground powder used for culinary purposes and cassia cinnamon is hard bark that is much tougher to crush or break. I tend to use cassia in magical workings as it is much cheaper to buy, and it burns well. For grinding to dress candles, Ceylon cinnamon is easier to use and has a sweeter aroma. Use cinnamon sticks whole, crushed into pieces, or ground, or as an essential oil

Cloves (Eugenia caryophyllus, Syzygium aromaticum, Caryophyllus aromaticus)

Magical Properties: Abundance, clarity, exorcism, love, money, prevents gossip, protection, repels negativity, stress relief, truth

Ruled By: Jupiter

Element: Fire

Energy: Masculine

Usage: Use dried cloves whole or crushed, or as an essential oil

Coffee (Coffee arabica)

Magical Properties: Clarity, divination, energy

Ruled By: Mars

Elements: Fire and water

Energy: Feminine

Usage: Use coffee beans whole or ground; instant coffee granules also work

Copal (Bursera odorata, Bursera fugaroides)

Magical Properties: Love, protection, purification

Ruled By: The sun and Jupiter

Zodiac Sign: Capricorn

Element: Fire

Energy: Masculine

Usage: Copal is a resin that can be ground to a powder or used as an essential oil

Coriander (Coriandrum sativum)

Magical Properties: Healing, health, love, peace, protection, releasing (especially negativity), wealth

Ruled By: Mars

Element: Fire

Energy: Masculine

Usage: Coriander seeds can be used, or leaves can be used dried or fresh; coriander essential oil is also available and made from the seeds

Cumin (Cumimum cyminum)

Magical Properties: Abundance, anti-theft, exorcism, fidelity, love, lust, peace, protection, success

Ruled By: Mars

Element: Fire

Energy: Masculine

Usage: Use cumin seeds or ground cumin powder

Daisy (Chrysanthemum leucanthemum, Bellis perennis)

Magical Properties: Courage, dreams, happiness, love, lust, protection, strength

Ruled By: Venus

Zodiac Signs: Cancer and Taurus

Element: Water

Energy: Feminine

Usage: Use the flowers and leaves fresh or dried, or as an essential oil

Dandelion (Taraxacum officinale)

Magical Properties: Abundance, divination, love, psychic abilities, wishes

Ruled By: Jupiter

Zodiac Sign: Taurus

Element: Air

Energy: Masculine

Usage: Use the flowers and leaves, fresh or dried, or the seed heads; buy dandelion-infused oil, either made with the flowers or leaves, or make your own by adding dandelion flowers to a base oil such as olive

Dragon's Blood (Dæmonorops draco, Dæmonorops propinquos)

Magical Properties: Dragon magic, happiness, love, power, protection

Ruled By: Mars

Zodiac Sign: Aries

Element: Fire

Energy: Masculine

Usage: Resin can be ground to a fine powder or sourced as an essential oil

Fennel (Fœniculum vulgare)

Magical Properties: Confidence, courage, fertility, healing, initiation, protection, purification

Ruled By: Mercury

Zodiac Signs: Leo, Virgo, and Aquarius

Element: Fire

Energy: Masculine

Usage: Use the flowers, leaves, and seeds, fresh or dried; also available as an essential oil

Frankincense (Boswellia sacra)

Magical Properties: Abundance, focus, love, purification, relaxation, spirituality

Ruled By: The sun

Zodiac Signs: Aries, Leo, and Aquarius

Element: Fire

Energy: Masculine

Usage: Resin can be ground into a powder or sourced as an essential oil

Geranium (Geranium maculatum, Pelargonium odoratissimum, Pelargonium × Hortorum)

Magical Properties: Aura cleansing, fertility, love, protection, socialisation

Ruled By: Venus

Zodiac Sign: Pisces

Element: Water

Energy: Feminine

Usage: Use the flowers or leaves of geranium (any of the *Pelargonium* family) fresh or dried; also available as an essential oil

Ginger (Zingiber officinale)

Magical Properties: Cleansing, consecrating, love, money, power, protection, success

Ruled By: Mars

Zodiac Sign: Aries

Element: Fire

Energy: Masculine

Usage: Use as an essential oil or as ground ginger powder; fresh ginger is good to add as a correspondence but does not grind well

Grass (Graminoids)

Magical Properties: Abundance, knot magic, psychic abilities, protection

Element: Earth

Usage: Use blades of grass or seed heads, fresh or dried

Hawthorn (Cratægus oxyacantha, Cratægus monogyna)

Magical Properties: Fairy magic, fertility, forgiveness, happiness, hope, love, protection, purification

Ruled By: Mars and Venus

Zodiac Sign: Sagittarius

Element: Fire

Energy: Masculine

Usage: Use the flowers, leaves, berries, and thorns, fresh or dried

Heather (Calluna vulgaris, Erica spp.)

Magical Properties: Cleansing, dreams, fairy magic, friendship, love, luck, protection, rain magic, shape-shifting, spirit work

Ruled By: Venus

Element: Water

Energy: Feminine

Usage: Use the flowers and leaves fresh or dried.

Holly (Ilex aquifolium, Ilex opaca)

Magical Properties: Balance, dreams, luck, protection, success

Ruled By: Mars and Saturn

Element: Fire

Energy: Masculine

Usage: Use the leaves, fresh or dried; berries can be used for magical purposes, but handle with care, as they are toxic to humans and pets

Honeysuckle (Lonicera caprifolium, Lonicera japonica, Lonicera periclymenum)

Magical Properties: Balance, lust, meditation, memory, prosperity, protection, psychic powers

Ruled By: Jupiter

Zodiac Signs: Gemini and Cancer

Element: Earth

Energy: Masculine

Usage: Use the flowers and leaves, dried or fresh, or as an essential oil

Jasmine (Jasminum grandiflorum, Jasminum officinale, Jasminum odoratissimum)

Magical Properties: Dreams, love, lust, meditation, money

Ruled By: Venus and the moon

Zodiac Sign: Cancer

Element: Water

Energy: Feminine

Usage: Use the flowers or leaves, dried or fresh, or as an essential oil

Juniper (Juniperus communes)

Magical Properties: Clarity, exorcism, healing, justice, love, protection, psychic abilities, purification, finding stolen items

Ruled By: The sun, Jupiter, and the moon

Zodiac Sign: Aries

Element: Fire

Energy: Masculine

Usage: Use the leaves and berries, fresh or dried, or as an essential oil

Lavender (Lavandula officinale, Lavandula vera)

Magical Properties: Clarity, fairy magic, happiness, love, peace, protection, sleep, strength

Ruled By: Mercury

Zodiac Signs: Leo and Gemini

Element: Air

Energy: Masculine

Usage: Use the flowers, leaves, and stems, dried or fresh; also available as an essential oil

Lemon (Citrus limon)

Magical Properties: Decisions, fidelity, friendship, happiness, love, moon magic, protection, purification, uplifting

Ruled By: The moon

Element: Water

Energy: Feminine

Usage: Use the leaves or peel, either fresh or dried; the juice and/or seeds; or as an essential oil

Lemon Balm (Melissa officinalis)

Magical Properties: Antidepressant, anxiety reducing, healing, love, memory, success

Ruled By: The moon and Venus

Zodiac Sign: Cancer

Element: Water

Energy: Feminine

Usage: Use the leaves, dried or fresh, or as an essential oil, often under the name Melissa

Lungwort (Pulmonaria officinalis)

Magical Properties: Calming, cleansing, healing, releasing

Ruled By: Mercury

Zodiac Signs: Taurus and Pisces

Element: Earth

Energy: Masculine

Usage: Use the flowers and leaves, dried or fresh

Marigold (Calendula officinalis)

Magical Properties: Dreams, happiness, luck, protection, psychic abilities, silencing gossip

Ruled By: The sun

Zodiac Sign: Leo

Element: Fire

Energy: Masculine

Usage: Use the flowers and leaves, fresh or dried, or as an essential oil

Marjoram (Origanum majorana)

Magical Properties: Happiness, health, love, marriage, overcoming grief, protection

Ruled By: Mercury

Zodiac Signs: Aries and Capricorn

Element: Air

Energy: Masculine

Usage: Use the leaves and flowers, fresh or dried, or as an essential oil

Mint (Mentha spp., Mentha aquatica, Mentha × piperita)

Magical Properties: Calming, cleansing, exorcism, healing, money, protection

Ruled By: Mercury and Venus

Zodiac Signs: Gemini, Taurus, Cancer, Leo, and Aquarius

Element: Air

Energy: Masculine

Usage: Use the leaves and stalks, fresh or dried, or as an essential oil. I have also had success with crushed-up peppermint candy!

Mustard (Brassica juncea, Brassica nigra, Sinapis spp.)

Magical Properties: Astral travel, clarity, faith, protection, psychic abilities, success

Ruled By: Mars

Element: Fire

Energy: Masculine

Usage: Use the dried seeds, mustard powder, or even mustard the condiment, which is a mixture of mustard seeds, water, salt, and a bit of lemon juice

Myrrh (Commiphora myrrha)

Magical Properties: Courage, Crone magic, healing, protection, purification, the Underworld

Ruled By: Mars and the sun

Zodiac Signs: Aries and Aquarius

Element: Water

Energy: Feminine

Usage: Resin can be ground into a powder for magical use; can also be sourced as an essential oil

Nettle (Urtica dioica)

Magical Properties: Exorcism, healing, lust, money, protection

Ruled By: Mars

Zodiac Signs: Scorpio and Aries

Element: Fire

Energy: Masculine

Usage: Use the leaves, fresh or dried; an infusion can easily be made by adding nettle leaves to a base oil such as olive

Nutmeg (Myristica fragrans)

Magical Properties: Fidelity, luck, money, protection

Ruled By: Jupiter

Zodiac Sign: Sagittarius

Element: Fire

Energy: Masculine

Usage: Use ground or as an essential oil

Oak (Quercus alba, Quercus robur, Quercus petræa)

Magical Properties: Fertility, healing, health, luck, money, power, protection, strength, vitality

Ruled By: The sun, Jupiter, and Mars

Zodiac Sign: Sagittarius

Elements: Fire and water

Energy: Masculine

Usage: Use the leaves, bark, and acorns, fresh or dried

Parsley (Petroselinum spp.)

Magical Properties: Fertility, happiness, lust, protection, purification, spirit work

Ruled By: Mercury

Zodiac Signs: Gemini and Leo

Element: Air

Energy: Masculine

Usage: Use the leaves, fresh or dried, or purchase parsley essential oil, made from the seeds

Patchouli (Pogostemon cablin)

Magical Properties: Balance, calm, earth magic, grounding, money, prosperity, protection, sex magic

Ruled By: Saturn

Zodiac Sign: Virgo

Element: Earth

Energy: Feminine

Usage: Use the leaves, dried or fresh, or as an essential oil

Pine (Pinus spp.)

Magical Properties: Abundance, centring, dragon magic, fertility, focus, healing, protection, purification, truth

Ruled By: Mars and Saturn

Zodiac Sign: Capricorn

Elements: Air and fire

Energy: Masculine

Usage: Use the pine needles, dried or fresh, or the bark; can also be found as an essential oil

Poppy (Papaver spp.)

Magical Properties: Easing grief, fertility, love, luck, money, rebirth, sleep

Ruled By: The moon, Mars, and Venus

Zodiac Sign: Capricorn

Element: Water

Energy: Feminine

Usage: Available as an essential oil, made from the seeds; use the petals, fresh or dried, or work with the seeds and seed heads

Rose (Rosa spp.)

Magical Properties: Abundance, death and rebirth, dreams, friendship, healing, knowledge, love, luck, mysteries, peace, protection, psychic powers

Ruled By: Venus and the moon

Zodiac Sign: Pisces

Element: Water

Energy: Feminine

Usage: Use the thorns and petals mainly, but the leaves also carry the magic of rose; also available as a nice essential oil

Rosemary (Rosmarinus officinalis)

Magical Properties: Exorcism, healing, love, lust, mental powers, protection, purification, sleep

Ruled By: The sun

Zodiac Sign: Aries

Element: Fire

Energy: Masculine

Usage: Use the leaves, stalks, and flowers, fresh or dried; also available as an essential oil

Rowan (Sorbus acuparia)

Magical Properties: Divination, fairy magic, healing, inspiration, love, power, protection, psychic abilities, spirituality, success

Ruled By: The sun and Mercury

Zodiac Sign: Sagittarius

Element: Fire

Energy: Masculine

Usage: Use the leaves, stalks, and berries, fresh or dried; raw rowan berries are toxic, so please handle with care

Sage (Salvia officinalis)

Magical Properties: Abundance, intuition, protection, purification, stimulation, success, wishes, wisdom

Ruled By: Jupiter

Zodiac Sign: Taurus and Sagittarius

Element: Air

Energy: Masculine

Usage: Use the leaves, fresh or dried, or source as an essential oil

Salt

Magical Properties: Cleansing, protection, purification

Ruled By: Earth

Element: Earth

Energy: Feminine

Usage: Any type of salt can be used for magical purpose; it does not need to be expensive—table salt works just as well as fancy salt

Sesame (Sesamum indicum)

Magical Properties: Energy, prosperity, protection, secrets, strength

Ruled By: The sun

Elements: Fire and earth

Energy: Masculine

Usage: Use the seeds in magical workings; sesame is used as a carrier oil

Star Anise (Illicium verum)

Magical Properties: Dreams, luck, protection, psychic abilities, purification, sleep, spirituality

Ruled By: Jupiter

Element: Air

Energy: Masculine

Usage: Use the dried spice in magical workings; also available as an essential oil

Sugar, White or Brown

Magical Properties: Love, making life sweet, protection

Ruled By: Venus

Element: Water

Energy: Feminine

Usage: Granulated sugar works the best

Sunflower (Helianthus annuus)

Magical Properties: Fertility, happiness, integrity, loyalty, luck, protection, truth, wishes

Ruled By: The sun

Zodiac Sign: Leo

Element: Fire

Energy: Masculine

Usage: Use the flowers, leaves, or seeds, dried or fresh; sunflower is a good oil to use as a carrier, but also works on its own

Tea (Camellia sinensis)

Magical Properties: Courage, meditation, prosperity, strength

Ruled By: The sun

Element: Fire

Energy: Masculine

Usage: Use the dried loose-leaf tea or empty a tea bag

Thyme (Thymus vulgaris, Thymus serpyllum)

Magical Properties: Beauty, courage, healing, health, love, peace, psychic abilities, purification, releasing, sleep

Ruled By: Venus

Element: Water

Energy: Feminine

Usage: Use the leaves, stalks, and flowers, fresh or dried; also available as an essential oil

Vanilla (Vanilla planifolia)

Magical Properties: Creativity, love, passion, sex magic, spirituality

Ruled By: Venus

Elements: Water and air

Energy: Feminine

Usage: Use vanilla pods, seeds, extract, or essential oil in magical workings

Witch Hazel (Hamamelis virginiana)

Magical Properties: Balance, divination, easing grief, protection

Ruled By: The sun and Saturn

Zodiac Sign: Capricorn

Element: Fire

Energy: Masculine

Usage: Use the leaves and bark, fresh or dried, or as an essential oil

Yarrow (*Achillea millefolium*)

Magical Properties: Courage, divination, dreams, exorcism, happiness, love, peace, psychic abilities, protection

Ruled By: Venus

Element: Water

Energy: Feminine

Usage: Use the flowers, leaves, and seeds, fresh or dried; also available as an essential oil

CHAPTER SEVEN

Timing and Energy

The timing of your spell work can really give your magic a kick. Spells can be tied to certain days of the week, planetary alignments, solar and lunar phases, and zodiac signs. Candles can be made, charged, or dressed to align with a particular moon phase or zodiac sign, adding yet another layer of power. With that being said, if you have a need to do a working right now…then do it. But, if you have a bit of time and want to add extra oomph to your magic, then wait to do your spell work until it aligns with your desired phase of the moon, day of the week, or planetary position.

Days of the Week

If you really want to get specific, perform your spell work on the day of the week that supports its intent.

Monday

Magical Properties: Ancestors, clarity, dreams, emotions, feminine energy, fertility, healing, illusions, intuition, moon magic, peace, protection, psychic abilities, travel, wisdom

Colour: White

Planet: Moon

Tuesday

Magical Properties: Challenges, confidence, courage, defence, fire magic, initiation, passion, personal power, protection, strength, success, wealth

Colour: Red

Planet: Mars

Wednesday

Magical Properties: Air magic, business matters, change, communication, creativity, cunning, fortune, guidance, luck, the arts, travel, wild magic

Colour: Purple

Planet: Mercury

Thursday

Magical Properties: Abundance, earth magic, finances, good health, grounding, growth, healing, luck, prosperity, protection, strength, wealth

Colour: Blue

Planet: Jupiter

Friday

Magical Properties: Attraction, beauty, fertility, friendship, growth, harmony, love, passion, relationships, romance, water magic

Colour: Green

Planet: Venus

Saturday

Magical Properties: Banishing, binding, cleansing, justice, protection, safety, spirituality, wisdom

Colour: Black

Planet: Saturn

Sunday

> **Magical Properties:** Acknowledgement, advancement, fame, hope, inspiration, personal achievements, promotion, prosperity, success, sun magic, victory, wealth
>
> **Colour:** Yellow
>
> **Planet:** Sun

Lunar Phases

The moon moves through all its phases within the span of approximately twenty-eight days. If you want to harness the moon's energy, I recommend inscribing the shape of the current moon phase onto your candle. Calendars and moon phase apps can be extremely helpful when it comes to gauging the moon's exact phase.

A word about the new and dark moon: Most moon calendars will show the dark moon as the first day of the new moon. For magical purposes, I separate them, as I believe they have different energies. The dark moon—when there is no moon to be seen at all—has a special magic of its own compared to the new moon, which I class as the first visible sliver of moon in the sky. It is up to you how you choose to work with them.

New Moon

> **Magical Properties:** Anything new (adventures, projects, etc.), beginnings, change, creativity, dreams, hope, ideas, inspiration, intention, intuition, luck, manifesting, opportunities, planning, potential, protection, wishes
>
> **Colours:** Green, orange, white
>
> **Herbs/Oils:** Basil, bay, cardamom, chamomile, chillies, cinnamon, jasmine, myrrh, nettle, nutmeg, oak, sage, vanilla

Waxing Crescent Moon

> **Magical Properties:** Abundance, attraction, business, career, communication, courage, creativity, determination, exploration, faith, fertility, flourishing, friendships, growth, healing, increasing, inspiration,

intention, knowledge, legal manifesting, love, luck, motivation, moving forward, power, prosperity, visualising, wishes

Colours: Orange, pink, blue

Herbs/Oils: Basil, cedar, cinnamon, coriander, fennel, ginger, honeysuckle, juniper, myrrh, pine, rosemary, thyme

First Quarter Moon

Magical Properties: Abundance, action, beauty, challenges, commitment, confidence, courage, creativity, elemental magic, emotions, family, fertility, friendships, growth, health, imagination, intuition, love, luck, manifesting, motivation, protection, psychic abilities, self-esteem, self-healing, self-love, spirituality, success, visualisation, wishes

Colours: Yellow, purple, blue

Herbs/Oils: Almond, benzoin, black pepper, cinnamon, dandelion, fennel, rowan, sage, sunflower

Waxing Gibbous Moon

Magical Properties: Adjustments, building, change, clarity, commitment, determination, editing, effort, energy, focus, go with the flow, goals, honing, openness, organisation, patience, persistence, potential, rebuilding, re-evaluating, refining, reviewing, routine, stamina

Colours: Blue, red, orange

Herbs/Oils: Chillies, cinnamon, coffee, poppy, rose, sesame

Full Moon

Magical Properties: Abundance, anxiety, blessings, celebration, chaos, confidence, commitment, communication, divination, encouragement, emotion, energy, forgiveness, fulfilment, gratitude, love, manifesting, power, psychic abilities, relationships, renewal, results, review, socialising, spell work of all kinds, success, truth, wildness, wisdom

Colours: White, purple, silver, red

Herbs/Oils: Basil, bergamot (orange), black pepper, chillies, chocolate, cinnamon, jasmine, mint, rose, thyme, vanilla, yarrow

Waning Gibbous Moon

Magical Properties: Acceptance, breaking habits, cleansing, curses, experience, letting go, protection, regrouping, relaxation, releasing, removing, repelling, reversing, separating, sharing, wisdom

Colours: White, black, light blue

Herbs/Oils: Bay, coriander, frankincense, jasmine, lemon, marjoram, mint, parsley, rosemary, sage, star anise, yarrow

Third Quarter Moon

Magical Properties: Adjustments, balance, breaking bad habits, challenges, cleansing, decisions, decreasing, direction, emotions, forgiveness, letting go, purification, reducing, re-evaluating, reflection, reorienting, release, rest, self-care

Colours: White, light blue, pink

Herbs/Oils: Chamomile, cinnamon, coriander, holly, honeysuckle, lemon, lungwort, patchouli, thyme, witch hazel

Waning Crescent Moon

Magical Properties: Acceptance, breaking bad habits, closure, dreams, endings, forgiveness, healing, hope, recuperating, reflection, rest, soothing, surrender

Colours: Blue, light green, pale yellow

Herbs/Oils: Bay, coriander, fennel, juniper, lungwort, mint, myrrh, nettle, pine, rosemary, star anise, thyme

Dark Moon

Magical Properties: Beauty, contemplation, health, inner work, introspection, looking ahead, personal improvement, planning, plotting, reflection, rejuvenation, self-analysis

Colours: Black, deep purple, dark blue

Herbs/Oils: Bay, benzoin, dandelion, dragon's blood, fennel, frankincense, ginger, hawthorn, heather, jasmine, myrrh, nutmeg, patchouli,
rosemary, sage, star anise, thyme

Solar Phases

If you prefer to work with solar magic, the sun has phases throughout the day
that can be used to add power to your spell work.

Sunrise

Magical Properties: Beginnings, change, cleansing, direction, employment, health, rebirth, renewal

The Morning

Magical Properties: Activity, building (projects and plans), courage,
expansion of ideas, growth, happiness, harmony, positive energy,
prosperity, resolutions, strength

High Noon

Magical Properties: Any spell work, health, knowledge, physical energy,
wisdom

The Afternoon

Magical Properties: Anything professional, business matters, communication, clarity, exploring, travel

Sunset

Magical Properties: Clarity, letting go, releasing, removing, stress
release, truth

Zodiac Signs

You may be familiar with zodiac signs. The sun moves through all twelve signs
once per year, staying in each sign for about one month. The general dates the
sun is in each zodiac sign are as follows, but do keep in mind that the dates
may fluctuate a bit depending on the year. Refer to an almanac or look online
for the exact date and time the sun will change signs.

If working a spell for yourself or another person you know, incorporate your zodiac sign(s) into the spell work somehow. Additionally, tying your spell work to the sign the sun is in can boost your magic's intent. I suggest inscribing the symbol of the current zodiac sign onto your candle. Zodiac signs can also be represented via colour magic; match the colour of your candle to the sign's corresponding colours. I have added some herb and oil suggestions so that you can dress and create your own astrological candles.

Aries ♈

Sun in Aries: 21 March to 19 April

Ruled By: Mars

Colours: Red, white, pink

Herbs/Oils: Bay, cinnamon, clove, dragon's blood, frankincense, ginger, juniper, marjoram, mustard, myrrh, nettle, rosemary

Taurus ♉

Sun in Taurus: 20 April to 20 May

Ruled By: Venus

Colours: Bright and vivid greens, red, yellow

Herbs/Oils: Daisy, dandelion, fern, iris, lungwort, mint, sage, sorrel, thyme

Gemini ♊

Sun in Gemini: 21 May to 20 June

Ruled By: Mercury

Colours: Bright yellow, red, blue

Herbs/Oils: Dill, honeysuckle, lavender, meadowsweet, mint, parsley, tansy, thyme

Cancer ♋

Sun in Cancer: 21 June to 22 July

Ruled By: The moon

Colours: White, silver, very pale blue, green, brown

Herbs/Oils: Catnip, daisy, dill, honeysuckle, hyssop, jasmine, lemon balm, mint, mugwort, star anise

Leo ♌

Sun in Leo: 23 July to 22 August

Ruled By: The sun

Colours: Gold, orange, dark yellow, red, green

Herbs/Oils: Bay, chamomile, dill, fennel, frankincense, lavender, marigold, mint, parsley, star anise, sunflower

Virgo ♍

Sun in Virgo: 23 August to 22 September

Ruled By: Mercury

Colours: Autumnal colours such as golden brown, deep greens and reds, gold, black

Herbs/Oils: Bergamot (orange), fennel, patchouli, sandalwood (red and white), valerian

Libra ♎

Sun in Libra: 23 September to 22 October

Ruled By: Venus

Colours: Pink, bright royal blue, black

Herbs/Oils: Bergamot, catnip, elder (leaves), elderflower, St. John's wort, thyme, violet

Scorpio ♏

Sun in Scorpio: 23 October to 21 November

Ruled By: Pluto

Colours: Dark reds, deep crimson, silver, brown, black

Herbs/Oils: Basil, blackthorn, cowslip, ivy, lily, nettle

Sagittarius ♐

Sun in Sagittarius: 22 November to 21 December

Ruled By: Jupiter

Colours: All shades of purple, gold, red

Herbs/Oils: Beech, birch, cedar, hawthorn, nutmeg, oak, rowan, sage, sandalwood (red and white)

Capricorn ♑

Sun in Capricorn: 22 December to 19 January

Ruled By: Saturn

Colours: Dark greens, dark brown and grey, red

Herbs/Oils: Benzoin, comfrey, copal, buttercup, marjoram, pine, plantain, poppy, sorrel, witch hazel

Aquarius ♒

Sun in Aquarius: 20 January to 18 February

Ruled By: Uranus

Colours: Bright blues, bright mixtures of colour, green

Herbs/Oils: Bergamot (orange), cypress, fennel, frankincense, mint, myrrh

Pisces ♓

Sun in Pisces: 19 February to 20 March

Ruled By: Neptune

Colours: Sea green, iridescent colours, white

Herbs/Oils: Fern, geranium, lemon verbena, lungwort, meadowsweet, rose, willow

The Moon and the Zodiac

The moon also travels through the zodiac, moving from one sign to the next every two or so days, meaning it travels through the entire zodiac every month. Moon calendars can tell you which sign the moon is in and when it will change signs. A simple but effective way to honour the moon's current sign is to inscribe the symbol for that zodiac sign onto your candle. This naturally boosts the energy of your spell.

The Moon in Aries

Magical Properties: Action, authority, bravery, courage, creativity, independence, initiative, job ventures, leadership, lust, movement, new projects, new skills, opportunities, overcoming obstacles, power, protection, purification, rebirth, renewal, strength, taking risks, willpower

The Moon in Taurus

Magical Properties: Comfort, connection, confidence, connection, creativity, determination, efficiency, financial security, glamour, growth, inner peace, love, organisation, patience, performance, practical matters, property, prosperity, rational thinking, relief, resourcefulness, sex, stability, staying power

The Moon in Gemini

Magical Properties: Adjustments, bad habits, communication, deals, disputes, energy, healing, ideas, learning, multitasking, negotiation, personal connections, short-distance travel, socialisation, teaching, transactions, transformation, uncrossing

The Moon in Cancer

Magical Properties: Abundance, children, compassion, divination, family, fertility, hearth, home, house hunting, inventiveness, moon magic, motherhood, nurturing, past lives, pregnancy, psychic abilities, romance, scrying, water magic

The Moon in Leo

Magical Properties: Authority, career, confidence, courage, creativity, dignity, entertainment, fame, fast money, fertility, the heart, honour, leadership, learning, loyalty, opportunity, strength, strong feelings, success, vitality

The Moon in Virgo

Magical Properties: Career, detail, education, employment, fertility, fitness, focus, hard work, harvest, healing, health, organisation, peace, planning, practicality, prosperity, purification, reaping reward, skill, stability, success

The Moon in Libra

Magical Properties: Artistic talent, balance, business, charm, compromise, contracts, decisions, diplomacy, eloquence, fairness, friendship, harmony, insight, justice, legal matters, love, marriage, partnerships, peace, social life, truth

The Moon in Scorpio

Magical Properties: Banishing, concentration, divination, emotion, energy, focus, healing, insight, loyalty, the occult, ownership, mysteries, passion, personal power, psychic development, renewal, secrets, sex magic, transformation

The Moon in Sagittarius

Magical Properties: Adventure, equality, goals, grounding, honesty, imagination, integrity, journeys, learning, long-distance travel, moderation, motion, new techniques, optimism, philosophy, publishing, study, tolerance, willpower, writing

The Moon in Capricorn

Magical Properties: Ambition, building, business, career, determination, discipline, drive, financial gain, logic, mysteries, organisation, patience, persistence, planning, politics, recognition, regulations, rules, secrets, spirituality, stability

The Moon in Aquarius

Magical Properties: Bad habits, choices, clarity, creativity, divination, empathy, freedom, friendships, goals, groups, idealism, independence, innovation, inspiration, intuition, invention, past lives, social life

The Moon in Pisces

Magical Properties: Action, art, banishing, care, compassion, creativity, deception, dream work, empathy, flow, imagination, inner work, instinct, intuition, luck, magic, past lives, progress, psychic abilities, romance, secrets, spirituality, transitions

Planets

The planets can also add a boost of magical energy to your spell work. Use a candle in a corresponding colour and carve the planet's symbol into the wax. If you want, you can add a separate candle to your spell that is also dressed with corresponding oils and herbs. No matter how many layers you choose to add, charge each ingredient with the energy of the planet as you are creating the candle. Here is a suggestion for a generic blessing you can use once you have created the candle:

> Planetary [planet name], bring your power
> Bless this candle for use at the magical hour

Jupiter ♃

Magical Properties: Abundance, authority, career, compassion, education, gain, good fortune, growth, healing, health, justice, knowledge, love, luck, peace, psychic skills, prosperity, protection, riches, spirituality, success, wealth, wisdom

Colours: Blue, indigo, purple, yellow

Herbs/Oils: Cedar, clove, dandelion, honeysuckle, hyssop, juniper, meadowsweet, nutmeg, oak, sage, sandalwood (red), star anise

Crystals: Amber, amethyst, black obsidian, citrine, goldstone, lapis lazuli, smoky quartz, sodalite

Mars ♂

Magical Properties: Aggression, ambition, assertion, competitiveness, conflict, courage, death, defence, discipline, energy, goals, independence, motivation, passion, power, problem-solving, protection, resolving arguments, revenge, sexuality, strength, success, victory, vitality, warrior energy, willpower

Colour: Red

Herbs/Oils: Basil, black pepper, blackthorn, cardamom, cumin, dragon's blood, ginger, hawthorn, mustard, myrrh, nettle, oak, pine, poppy, tobacco

Crystals: Bloodstone, garnet, green aventurine, pyrite, red jasper, tourmaline, unakite

Mercury ☿

Magical Properties: Business, communication, deception, divination, dream work, education, employment, exchange, gain, healing, insight, learning, magic, memory, protection, speed, study, technology, teaching, theft, travel, understanding

Colours: Deep yellow, bright orange, multicoloured

Herbs/Oils: Bergamot (orange), dill, fennel, fern, lavender, lemon verbena, lungwort, marjoram, mint, parsley, rowan, sandalwood (white), yew

Crystals: Agate, blue lace agate, green aventurine, jasper

Moon ☾

Magical Properties: Birth, change, compassion, emotion, dispelling negativity, divination, family, fertility, gratitude, health, healing, illusion, lost items, love, lunar magic, manifesting, mysteries, protection, riches, spirituality, transformation, travel, water magic

Colours: White, silver, grey

Herbs/Oils: Hyssop, ivy, jasmine, juniper, lemon balm, mugwort, poppy, rose, sandalwood (white), willow

Crystals: Clear quartz, grey jasper, labradorite, moonstone, moss agate, rose quartz, selenite

Saturn ♄

Magical Properties: Binding, boundaries, focus, dispelling negativity, good fortune, healing, home, inner work, intellect, manifesting, meditation, money, resilience, power, protection, responsibility, safety, structure, success in business

Colours: Black, grey

Herbs/Oils: Blackthorn, comfrey, cypress, foxglove ivy, pansy, patchouli, pine, witch hazel, yew

Crystals: Black obsidian, hematite, smoky quartz

Sun ☉

Magical Properties: Ambition, clarity, communication, confidence, creativity, diplomacy, energy, fertility, friendships, gain, goals, growth, harmony, healing, health, hope, inspiration, joy, leadership, love, manifesting, masculine energy, peace, power, prosperity, renewal, solar magic, success, transformation, truth, wealth, will

Colours: Gold or yellow

Herbs/Oils: Bay, benzoin, bergamot (orange), cedar, chamomile, cinnamon, copal, frankincense, juniper, marigold, myrrh, oak, rosemary, rowan, sunflower, witch hazel

Crystals: Amber, carnelian, citrine, clear quartz, orange calcite, pyrite, sunstone, tiger's eye

Venus ♀

Magical Properties: Attraction, beauty, creativity, education, emotion, fertility, good fortune, happiness, harmony, inspiration, jealousy, joy, love, lust, money, passion, peace, pleasure, prosperity, relationships, self-confidence, sexuality, success, victory

Colours: Green, pastels

Herbs/Oils: Benzoin, cardamom, catnip, daisy, foxglove, geranium, hawthorn, jasmine, lemon balm, mint, mugwort, plantain, poppy, rose, sandalwood (red), thyme, yarrow

Crystals: Celestite, goldstone, green jasper, lapis lazuli, malachite, rose quartz, sodalite, tourmaline, turquoise, unakite

CHAPTER EIGHT

Additional Correspondences

The magical world offers a variety of different signs, symbols, and images that can bring extra power to your magic. Some of these draw upon our sense of sight and what we associate with certain symbols; others are drawn from ancient languages or means of communication. This chapter focuses on all sorts of visual images.

Sigils are a particular favourite of mine. When you create a sigil, you are creating something that is full of power and intent that is also secret—no one knows what it means except you. That adds a whole other dimension to your magical working. There is mystery to a secret symbol!

Other images, such as runes and tarot cards, will also be discussed in this chapter. You don't need to be able to read tarot cards or runes to use them in candle magic; understanding the keywords for each is enough. My hope is that after you've read this chapter, you will experiment with different tools and see what a difference they make in your magic.

Sigils

Sigils are magical symbols, carved or drawn, that bring power. Sigils are personal. Each one is unique to its creator, and each will be different. A sigil represents exactly what you want to bring into your spell work.

Practice

Creating a Sigil

There are several ways to create a sigil. Here is one way.

You will need

    Piece of paper

    Pen

Before creating a sigil, you need an intent and a phrase that sums up your intended outcome. Keep it positive and simple. For example, if you were working a money draw spell, you could start with the phrase *Money, come to me.*

The letters of the phrase will create the sigil, but they need to be simplified first. Remove all the vowels and any letters that are duplicated. Once you have done so, you have the letters that will be used in your sigil. Building on my previous example, *Money, come to me* becomes *mnyct.*

Next, grab the pen and paper and write down the letters to be used in your sigil. Create a pleasing image using these letters. Be guided by your intuition and be as creative (or as simple) as you'd like. You could draw the letters one on top of the other, or you could space them out and link them together somehow. It may take a few tries for you to land on a sigil design that you really like.

Once you have completed your design, your sigil is complete! To use the sigil in candle magic, you could carve it on the side of the candle, or you could pin a small piece of paper with the sigil drawn on it to the candle.

m∅n¢y c∅m¢ t∅ m¢

m n y c t

Sigil

Practice
∽

Magic Circle Sigil

This type of sigil uses the letters of the alphabet and a statement, just like the previous exercise. This time, though, we're adding in the magic of a circle. Circles have their own energy and can bring in a continuous, never-ending cycle of magic.

You will need

    Piece of paper

    Pen

Start by writing out your request. For my example, I am going to use the same intent as before: *Money, come to me*. Remove the vowels and any duplicated letters. (In my case, I end up with *mnyct*.)

m n y c t

Circle Sigil

Next, draw a circle on the piece of paper. Rather than drawing a circle freehand, I find it easier to trace around the base of a glass or cup.

Then, write out the alphabet, keeping all the letters along the inside edge of the circle as evenly spaced as possible.

Once the circle and alphabet are complete, remember your phrase. Draw a straight line connecting the first letter of your shortened phrase to the second letter, the second to the third, and so on. So, for my example, I would draw a line from *m* to *n*, then from the *n* to *y*, from the *y* to the *c*, and so on, continuing until I had connected all the letters.

Look at the shape you have created with the straight lines. That is your sigil! Transfer the sigil onto a candle. You do not need to add the circle or the letters, just the shape the lines created.

Freestyle Sigil

Alternatively, you can let your creative instincts run wild and go freestyle. Take any symbols that represent your intent and make a design from them. Add in lines, swirls, dots, doodles, or whatever you feel inclined to draw. Focus on the outcome and your goals and desires whilst you are creating the sigil. When you feel it is finished, it can be transferred onto a candle.

In the example shown here, I worked with the intent of money drawing and incorporated a pound sign (£), the rune Fehu, and the ogham Duir/Oak, along with a four-leaf clover.

Freestyle Sigil Example

Shapes and Symbols

There are so many shapes and symbols out there that it can be hard to know which to use in your spell work. Here are some suggestions, but go with what works for you. Ultimately, the symbol must have a clear meaning to you. Some symbols have a universal meaning, such as a heart representing love, but others might have a very personal meaning to you.

Awen: Inspiration, triple aspect of deity, creation, truth

Circle: Unity, protection, cycle of life, full moon, sun

Heart: Love, romance, passion, happiness, harmony

Smiley Face: Happiness

Pentagram: Protection, the elements

Pound or Dollar Sign: Money, prosperity, wealth

Sun: Solar magic

Moon: Lunar magic

Four-Leaf Clover: Luck

X: Protection, multiplication, a kiss, signature, treasure

Triquetra: Triple goddess, land, sea and sky, the mind

Spiral: Solar magic, journeys

Triskelion: Fertility, mother goddess, interconnectedness

Solar Cross: Solar magic, the seasons

Period/Full Stop: Endings, a destination spot

Arrow: Directions, moving forward

Cross: Decisions, directions, meeting place, balance

Wavy Lines: Water, ocean, movement

Square: Boundaries, binding, secrets

Crescent: Depending on which way it is facing, waxing or waning moon

Horseshoe: Luck, protection

Eye: All-seeing, divination, intuition, spirituality, psychic abilities, protection

Infinity: Endless, eternal time

Wheel: Journey, travel, speed, movement, change; can also represent a shield and, therefore, protection

Key or Keyhole: Unlocking doors, secrets, revealing, truth, Otherworld access, protection, insight

Scales: Balance, justice

God: A simple circle with a semi-circle on top represents the God and masculine energy

Goddess: A simple, curved bodily shape with arms raised represents the Goddess and feminine energy

The Elements: If you want to bring in the energy of the elements, use their triangle symbols:

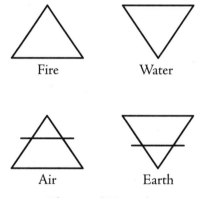

Fire   Water

Air   Earth

Elemental Triangles

Runes

Although we do not know the true history of the runes, we do know that they are an alphabet. Each rune represents a letter, but they are so much more than that. Runes are most often used in divination, but I present them here to be used within candle magic. Runes can be carved into a candle or written on a petition to bring a surge of power to your spell.

Here is a list of the runes and their magical meanings, but keep in mind that this is a general list. You may develop a personal connection to the runes and find that your meanings are slightly different than mine.

Fehu ᚠ

Properties: Abundance, achievement, career, confidence, fertility, good fortune, harmony, health, luck, material possessions, money, recognition, spiritual development, wealth

Elements: Fire and earth

Uruz ᚢ

Properties: Change, courage, creativity, energy, freedom, goals, gratitude, happiness, harmony, healing, health, independence, luck, organisation, passion, power, strength, vitality

Element: Earth

Thurisaz ᚦ

Properties: Decisions, luck, opportunity, protection, strength

Element: Fire

Ansuz ᚨ

Properties: Clarity, communication, insight, inspiration, knowledge, spirituality, teaching, truth, wisdom

Element: Air

Raidho ᚱ

Properties: Action, change, decisions, direction, fate, journey, movement, transformation, travel

Element: Air

Kenaz ᚲ

Properties: Change, creativity, inspiration, knowledge, passion, revelation, support, teaching, vision

Elements: Water and fire

Gebo X

Properties: Abundance, connection, contracts, freedom, happiness, luck, possibilities, prosperity, relationships, support, talent

Elements: Air and water

Wunjo ᚹ

Properties: Happiness, harmony, health, hope, joy, prosperity, recharging, success

Element: Earth

Hagalaz ᚺ

Properties: Challenges, change, disruption, focus, lessons, release

Elements: Earth and water

Naudhiz ᚾ

Properties: Achievements, change, direction, innovation, need, obstacles, survival

Elements: Earth and fire

Isa ᛁ

Properties: Calming, grounding, meditation, relaxation

Elements: Water and fire

Jera ᛃ

Properties: Achievements, completion, growth, happiness, harvest, justice, motivation, patience, peace, prosperity, seasons, success, transitions

Elements: Air and earth

Eihwaz ᛇ

Properties: Beginnings, death, endurance, protection, rebirth, reliability, renewal, spirituality, strength, stability, transformation, trust, wisdom

Elements: Earth, air, fire, and water

Pertho ᛈ

Properties: Ancestors, community, creativity, family, friendship, intuition, luck, magic, meditation, mysteries, psychic abilities, rebirth, spirit work

Element: Water

Algiz ᛉ

Properties: Defence, dispelling negativity, protection, security, wisdom

Element: Air

Sowilo ᛊ

Properties: Banishing, beginnings, confidence, direction, energy, good fortune, happiness, healing, health, leadership, power, rebirth, spirituality, strength, success, sun magic, victory

Element: Fire

Teiwaz ᛏ

Properties: Confidence, courage, honour, justice, protection, sacrifice, strength, truth, victory, warrior energy, wisdom

Element: Air

Berkana ᛒ

Properties: Beginnings, feminine energy, fertility, Goddess, growth, luck, motherhood, nurturing, opportunity, patience, planning, purification, release, success

Element: Earth

Ehwaz ᛖ

Properties: Change, connections, fears, initiation, journey, movement, partnerships, spirituality, strength, success, transformation, transitions

Element: Earth

Mannaz ᛗ

Properties: Balance, change, community, cooperation, family, focus, friendship, happiness, identity, insight, responsibility, self-understanding, skills, support, teamwork

Element: Air

Laguz ᚱ

Properties: Cleansing, emotion, energy, flexibility, flow, intuition, journey, meditation, movement, mysteries, psychic abilities, spirituality, spirit work, strength, water magic

Element: Water

Inguz ◇

Properties: Beginnings, confidence, creativity, fertility, grounding, growth, harmony, health, intuition, motivation, peace, relaxation, spirituality, unity

Elements: Earth and water

Dagaz ᛞ

Properties: Abundance, awakening, balance, change, clarity, determination, enlightenment, hope, manifesting, opportunity, prosperity, spirituality, success, transformation, transition, wealth

Elements: Earth and air

Othila ᛟ

Properties: Abundance, ancestors, arguments, balance, breaking cycles, communication, community, family, friendships, grounding, inspiration, harmony, home, peace, possessions, prosperity, relationships, spirituality, wealth

Element: Earth

Ogham

The ogham is an ancient system of symbols used for divination. It was once thought to be a tree alphabet. The symbols can be used in candle magic to add a layer of magical energy. Carve your ogham symbol into a candle or draw it on a petition.

Beith/Birch ⊤

> **Properties:** Beginnings, change, cleansing, creativity, hope, initiation, protection, purification
>
> **Elements:** Air and water

Luis/Rowan ⊤⊤

> **Properties:** Creativity, defence, healing, inspiration, magic, psychic abilities, power, protection, success
>
> **Element:** Earth

Fearn/Alder ⊤⊤⊤

> **Properties:** Challenges, confidence, courage, creativity, decisions, dream work, easing fear, emotions, guidance, intuition, knowledge, protection, spiritual guidance
>
> **Elements:** Water and fire

Saille/Willow ⊤⊤⊤⊤

> **Properties:** Balance, divination, dreams, emotions, fertility, flexibility, healing, inspiration, intuition, love, moon magic, protection, soothing grief, water magic
>
> **Element:** Water

Nuinn/Ash ⊤⊤⊤⊤⊤

> **Properties:** Balance, change, courage, fate, friendship, growth, harmony, healing, health, manifesting, organisation, peace, protection, renewal, transition
>
> **Element:** Air

Huathe/Hawthorn ⊥

Properties: Clearing negativity, fertility, happiness, healing, insight, intuition, overcoming obstacles, patience, protection, relaxation, wisdom

Element: Air

Duir/Oak ⊥⊥

Properties: Courage, endurance, healing, health, justice, leadership, luck, money, protection, security, strength, trust, wisdom

Element: Earth

Tinne/Holly ⊥⊥⊥

Properties: Bravery, creativity, defence, dream work, harmony, luck, patience, perspective, protection, sacrifice, skills, transformation

Elements: Earth and fire

Coll/Hazel ⊥⊥⊥⊥

Properties: Divination, dreams, enlightenment, fertility, insight, inspiration, intuition, knowledge, luck, meditation, protection, rituals, wisdom, wishes

Elements: Air and water

Quert/Apple ⊥⊥⊥⊥⊥

Properties: Connection, decisions, harmony, healing, health, love, magic, meditation, prosperity, renewal, rest, spirituality

Element: Water

Muinn/Bramble ⟋

Properties: Abundance, communication, creativity, fun, goals, growth, harvest, healing, persuasion, protection, relaxation, rest, spirituality, truth, wealth

Elements: Air and earth

Gort/Ivy ⌗

Properties: Abundance, banishing, binding, development, friendship, gratitude, growth, harmony, healing, protection, rest, restriction, strength, support, tenacity, wild magic

Element: Air

Ngeadal/Broom ⌗

Properties: Calming, cleansing, divination, harmony, healing, health, meditation, purification, strength, vitality

Element: Water

Straif/Blackthorn ⌗

Properties: Banishing negativity, challenges, conflict, courage, energy, exorcism, hope, protection, purification, secrets, spirit work

Elements: Air and fire

Ruis/Elder ⌗

Properties: Jealousy, karma, knowledge, magic, obsession, rebirth, renewal, shadow work, sleep, transformation, wisdom

Element: Fire

Ailm/Pine +

Properties: Ancestors, attraction, clarity, connection, direction, expression, enlightenment, fertility, growth, healing, intuition, joy, perception, purification, spirituality, understanding

Element: Fire

Onn/Gorse ╫

Properties: Abundance, direction, gratitude, harvest, hope, lust, money, movement, removing obstacles, sexuality, spirituality, travel, vitality

Elements: Air and fire

Ur/Heather ⫲

Properties: Cleansing, connection, death, cycles, fairy magic, love, luck, magic, memory, partnership, passion, relationships, removing negativity, respect, spirituality

Element: Fire

Edhadh/Aspen ⫲

Properties: Bravery, connection, defeating fear, divine communication, divination, endurance, enlightenment, flexibility, insight, overcoming worry, perception, prosperity, protection, releasing negativity, shadow work, truth, wealth

Element: Air

Idho/Yew ⫲

Properties: Ancestors, beginnings, cycles, death, life, meditation, memory, transition, wisdom

Element: Earth

Number Correspondences

Below are the intents I associate with numbers. If you are drawn to numerology, do investigate, as it is a fascinating subject!

1: Connection, control, determination, efficiency, goals, grounding, harmony, independence, innovation, leadership, life force, motivation, personal power, self-sufficiency, Source, the Universe

2: Balance, cooperation, duality, feminine energy, grace, influence, intuition, light and dark, partnerships, peace, polarity, power, protection, relationships, support

3: Action, connection of the body, communication, creativity, energy, health, mind and spirit, interaction, optimism, socialising, spirituality, the Triple Goddess, the Triple God

4: Cardinal directions, compassion, creativity, earth magic, elements, emotion, foundations, hard work, loyalty, organisation, patience, practicality, seasons, strength

5: Adventure, chaos, change, flexibility, independence, movement, psychic abilities, senses, socialising, spirituality, transformation

6: Caring, compassion, empathy, harmony, healing, love, nurturing, partnerships, power, protection, responsibility, romance, security, solar energy, support

7: Curiosity, feminine energy, inner work, intellect, intuition, lunar energy, mysteries, perception, spirituality, water magic, wisdom

8: Accomplishments, authority, balance, communication, dedication, material goals, messages, power, prosperity, success

9: Acceptance, compassion, completion, experience, fulfilment, kindness, spirituality, transition, truth, wisdom

Practice

The Power of Thirteen Spell

This spell was originally written to be worked on Friday the thirteenth, but it can be worked to bring in the energy of thirteen by working the spell on the thirteenth day of any month, or even at the thirteenth hour of the day (1:00 p.m.). This spell could be adapted to work with any number and then cast on the corresponding date of the month. The intent of my spell was to use the power to bring in thirteen positive energies, such as happiness and balance, but you can adapt it to suit your own intentions by swapping out some of mine and adding your own.

This spell has the most ingredients I have ever used in a spell, but I designed it this way because I wanted thirteen of everything. Originally, I followed my intuition and went with crystals and herbs that I selected from my cupboard, knowing they were what I needed rather than looking up their meanings.

You will need

13 candles, one for each intent: love, success, prosperity, friendship, stability, protection, happiness, health, clarity, intuition, peace, balance, and abundance

13 crystals:

    Rose quartz for love

    Goldstone for success

    Pyrite for prosperity

    Turquoise for friendship

    Hematite for stability

    Obsidian for protection

    Sunstone for happiness

    Labradorite for health

    Clear quartz for clarity

    Selenite for intuition

    Celestite for peace

    Moonstone for balance

    Lapis lazuli for abundance

13 herbs:

    Rose petals for love

    Cinnamon for success

    Basil for prosperity

    Heather for friendship

    Soil for stability

    Salt for protection

    Sunflower for happiness

    Thyme for health

    Cardamom for clarity

    Sage for intuition

    Lavender for peace

    Chamomile for balance

    Cloves for abundance

Charge each candle, crystal, and herb with your intent before arranging them on your altar. Place them in a design that you feel is right; trust your intuition. I placed all of mine on a round, silver tray, coincidentally representing the moon (there being thirteen moons in a year).

Now, light each candle. As you light each one, say the following chant:

> *The power of thirteen, may you bring to me*
> *All the good things in life that be*
> *Include within, gratitude and thanks*
> *Allow me to receive all by giving freely*
> *Life is good, life is blessed*
> *Join with me, wishing everyone all the best*

You will repeat the chant a total of thirteen times.

Once the spell is done, keep the thirteen crystals on your altar for a while. Sprinkle the herbs onto your garden or some grass, or create a loose incense blend from them.

Personal Notes

The candles I used were a mixture of tea lights and small votives in glass jars, as these all stood safely on a tray. However, if you'd prefer, you can use spell or beeswax candles.

I picked the thirteen crystals for this spell purely by intuition; most of them were small tumbled stones I had in my collection. If you have a stash of crystals, trust your intuition for which ones to choose. If you do not have enough (or any) crystals, you could use pebbles or shells, or think creatively and use things from your kitchen cupboards, such as nuts, dried beans, or dried pasta twists. If you do not want to, you do not need to use any at all; this spell can be worked with just candles.

The herbs I used were whole; I did not grind them. I did not dress the candles with the herbs, either—I just placed them in and around the candles and crystals. If you'd prefer, you could use just one type of herb, chopped into thirteen pieces.

Tarot Cards

Tarot cards are a great focal point for any spell working. Choose the card that best represents your intent and place it in front of your candle spell, or set it behind your candle. Use the card you chose to help you visualise your goal or desire. After working a spell, I cleanse the tarot card by passing it through incense smoke, then return it to the pack. I keep a tarot deck specifically for spell work, one that I don't use for readings. I also have an oracle deck that I use just for spell work.

What is the difference between a tarot deck and an oracle deck? Oracle decks are more customisable. The number of cards, card messages, and artwork will depend on the deck. While the messages of an oracle deck may differ, each card usually has one or more keywords on it. Tarot decks have a set number of cards (seventy-eight), and each card has a standard meaning. Most also include certain symbols or imagery, no matter who created the art. Here are some of my suggestions for cards that may correspond with your magical intent.

Balance: The Lovers, Justice, Temperance, Two of Swords, Four of Wands, Two of Cups

Binding: Temperance, Two of Swords, Eight of Swords, the Hanged Man

Changes: Wheel of Fortune, the Magician, Eight of Wands, Judgement

Clarity, Insight and Truth: The High Priestess, the Lovers, Justice, the Tower, the Moon, Ace of Swords, Knight of Wands, Seven of Cups, Queen of Cups

Communication: Five of Swords, Two of Swords, the High Priestess, Knight of Swords, Five of Wands, Seven of Swords, Four of Cups, Page of Swords, King of Swords

Courage: The Star, Strength, the Chariot

Cursing: The Devil, the Tower

Decisions and Direction: Justice, the Hermit, the Star, the Lovers

Fertility: The Sun, Ten of Cups, Ace of Wands

Friendship: Three of Cups, Two of Cups, Knight of Cups

Gratitude: Ten of Pentacles, Nine of Cups, Six of Pentacles, the Sun, Six of Wands, Four of Swords, the Empress, Strength, Ace of Cups

Happiness: The Sun, the World, Ace of Cups

Healing: Strength, the World, the Magician, the Sun, the Star, Three of Cups

Inspiration and Creativity: The Magician, the Sun, Ace of Wands

Love: The Lovers, Knight of Cups, the Star

Luck: The World, the Star, Wheel of Fortune

New Beginnings: The Fool, the Emperor, the World, the Chariot, the Hermit, Death, the Sun, Two of Pentacles, Ten of Swords, Ace of Wands, Knight of Wands, Four of Cups, Eight of Cups

Peace and Harmony: The Star, Five of Cups, the Hermit, Temperance

Psychic Abilities: The High Priestess, the Devil, the Moon

Protection: The Star, the Chariot, Temperance, Four of Wands

Prosperity: Ten of Pentacles, Knight of Pentacles, Page of Pentacles, Six of Pentacles, Ace of Pentacles

Removing Obstacles: Two of Cups, the Chariot, Strength

Releasing: The Moon, Judgement, the World

Strength: Strength, Six of Wands, the Emperor, the Star, the Lovers, Nine of Wands, Seven of Wands, Six of Swords, any of the Kings

Stress Relief: The Hanged Man, Ace of Cups, Temperance, Four of Cups

Success: The Chariot, Six of Wands, Five of Wands

Transformation: Temperance, the World, Judgement, the Magician, Strength, the High Priestess, the Chariot

Uncrossing/Unhexing: Any of the following cards, but turn them upside down so they are reversed: Temperance, Two of Swords, Eight of Swords, the Hanged Man

Crystals

Each crystal has an individual energy. It is by tapping into that energy that we discover what magic the crystal can help us with. I love to use tumbled stones in my candle magic. Just one tumbled stone placed in front of a candle spell will be charged with that spell's intent and can be carried with you afterwards. Crystals can also be arranged in a circle around a candle to add their energy to spell work. Trust your intuition (and your budget) when choosing which crystals to use. Here are some of my suggestions.

Agate (Banded, Brown, and Black)

Magical Properties: Balance, binding, clarity, cursing, gratitude, happiness, harmony, healing, insight, peace, protection, strength, success, truth

Element: Fire

Planet: Mercury

Amber

Magical Properties: Balance, clarity, cleansing, healing, insight, psychic abilities, purifying, success, truth

Element: Fire

Planet: Sun

Amethyst

Magical Properties: Change, clarity, gratitude, happiness, harmony, insight, luck, peace, protection, success, transformation, truth, uncrossing, unhexing

Element: Water

Planet: Jupiter

Black Tourmaline

Magical Properties: Balance, change, cursing, friendship, happiness, harmony, peace, protection, releasing, transformation

Element: Earth

Planets: Venus, Mars

Bloodstone

Magical Properties: Clarity, healing, insight, prosperity, protection, strength, truth, uncrossing, unhexing

Elements: Earth, fire

Planet: Mars

Blue Lace Agate

Magical Properties: Cleansing, communication, purifying

Element: Water

Planet: Mercury

Carnelian

Magical Properties: Confidence, courage, cursing, decisions, direction, harmony, love, luck, peace, protection, success, uncrossing, unhexing

Element: Fire

Planet: Sun

Celestite

Magical Properties: Clarity, communication, happiness, harmony, healing, insight, peace, spirit work, truth

Elements: Air, water

Planets: Venus, Neptune

Citrine

Magical Properties: Change, clarity, confidence, courage, gratitude, happiness, healing, insight, psychic abilities, success, transformation, truth

Element: Fire

Planets: Sun, Jupiter

Clear Quartz

Magical Properties: Balance, clarity, cleansing, communication, decisions, direction, healing, insight, protection, psychic abilities, purifying, spirit work, strength, truth

Elements: Fire, water

Planets: Sun, moon

Fluorite

Magical Properties: Balance, cleansing, communication, confidence, courage, decisions, direction, gratitude, harmony, healing, peace, purifying, releasing, removing obstacles

Elements: Water, air

Planet: Neptune

Garnet

Magical Properties: Cleansing, purifying, spirit work

Element: Fire

Planet: Mars

Goldstone

Magical Properties: Clarity, confidence, courage, decisions, direction, insight, luck, prosperity, success, truth

Elements: Earth, fire

Planets: Venus, Jupiter

Green Aventurine

Magical Properties: Balance, decisions, direction, gratitude, happiness, harmony, healing, luck, peace, prosperity, psychic abilities

Element: Air

Planets: Mercury, Mars

Hematite

Magical Properties: Balance, communication, decisions, direction, healing, protection, removing obstacles, strength, uncrossing, unhexing

Elements: Earth, fire

Planet: Saturn

Jasper

Magical Properties: Balance, confidence, courage, cursing, happiness, harmony, healing, peace, releasing, uncrossing, unhexing

Elements: Earth, air, fire (depending on colour)

Planets: Venus, Mercury, Uranus, moon, Mars (depending on colour)

Labradorite

Magical Properties: Change, clarity, cleansing, confidence, courage, decisions, direction, healing, insight, luck, protection, psychic abilities, purifying, strength, success, transformation, truth

Element: Water

Planets: Earth, moon, Uranus

Lapis Lazuli

Magical Properties: Clarity, confidence, courage, decisions, direction, harmony, insight, love, luck, peace, removing obstacles, success, truth

Element: Water

Planets: Venus, Jupiter

Malachite

Magical Properties: Change, clarity, harmony, healing, insight, love, new beginnings, peace, prosperity, psychic abilities, releasing, strength, success, transformation, truth, uncrossing, unhexing

Element: Earth

Planet: Venus

Moonstone

Magical Properties: Balance, clarity, cleansing, confidence, communication, courage, fertility, gratitude, harmony, healing, insight, love, new beginnings, peace, psychic abilities, purifying, truth

Element: Water

Planet: Moon

Moss Agate

Magical Properties: Cleansing, fertility, friendship, new beginnings, prosperity, purifying, releasing

Element: Earth

Planet: Moon

Obsidian

Magical Properties: Binding, cleansing, cursing, protection, purifying, releasing, removing obstacles, spirit work, strength

Elements: Fire, earth, water

Planets: Jupiter, Saturn

Orange Calcite

Magical Properties: Change, clarity, cleansing, confidence, courage, harmony, insight, peace, purifying, releasing, transformation, truth

Element: Earth

Planet: Sun

Pebble/Hag Stone

Magical Properties: Fertility, protection

Elements: Earth, water

Planet: Earth

Pyrite

Magical Properties: Clarity, confidence, communication, courage, cursing, decisions, direction, insight, luck, prosperity, protection, psychic abilities, releasing, removing obstacles, strength, success, truth

Element: Fire

Planets: Mars, sun

Rose Quartz

Magical Properties: Balance, cleansing, fertility, friendship, happiness, harmony, healing, love, luck, peace, purifying, success

Elements: Earth, water

Planets: Venus, moon

Selenite

Magical Properties: Balance, clarity, cleansing, decisions, direction, healing, insight, love, protection, psychic abilities, purifying, spirit work, success, truth

Element: Water

Planet: Moon

Smoky Quartz

Magical Properties: Clarity, decisions, direction, insight, luck, releasing, removing obstacles, truth, uncrossing, unhexing

Element: Earth

Planets: Saturn, Jupiter

Sodalite

Magical Properties: Confidence, courage, friendship, harmony, love, peace, psychic abilities, releasing

Element: Water

Planets: Jupiter, Venus

Sunstone

Magical Properties: Balance, clarity, decisions, direction, gratitude, happiness, harmony, healing, insight, love, luck, peace, prosperity, protection, strength, truth

Element: Fire

Planet: Sun

Tiger's Eye

Magical Properties: Balance, binding, clarity, confidence, courage, healing, insight, luck, prosperity, protection, psychic abilities, releasing, removing obstacles, strength, success, truth, uncrossing, unhexing

Elements: Fire, earth

Planet: Sun

Turquoise

Magical Properties: Balance, clarity, cleansing, communication, cursing, friendship, harmony, insight, love, luck, peace, protection, psychic abilities, purifying, truth

Element: Earth

Planets: Venus, Neptune

Unakite

Magical Properties: Change, confidence, courage, decisions, direction, happiness, harmony, love, peace, releasing, strength, success, transformation

Element: Water

Planets: Mars, Venus

PART III
CANDLE MAGIC SPELLS

CHAPTER NINE

Before You Begin

Most spells work from a basic structure. I look at a spell like a recipe: you have a list of ingredients, but you can tweak it to suit what you have on hand or what your personal tastes are. In the following pages, I will provide a basic method for how to work the magic. I'll also include lots of different ingredients to choose from. This way you have some structure *and* inspiration, so you can tailor the spell to fit your needs.

Unless otherwise stated, the spells in this part of the book work best with small spell candles or rolled beeswax candles. Tea lights or votives could be used but will take much longer to burn out.

Colour options are given as an idea for the colour of candle to use for each intent. Colour can also be brought in with the use of altar cloths, candleholders, ink, or another magical tool.

Suggestions for carrier oils, dressing oils, and herbs are also given. Pick and choose whether you want to dress your candle with oil and/or herbs.

The option to carve symbols onto the candle is included. This can be omitted, or the symbol can be replaced with your own sigil design.

Runes and ogham that correspond to each intent have been included. These can be carved onto the candle or written on a petition.

Petition suggestions are given. If you choose to write one, the petition can be pinned to the candle, placed underneath it, or set in front. The petition can also be lit from the candle flame and burnt in a safe container.

Chant suggestions are given. These can be said aloud or used as inspiration for your own chant.

Corresponding numbers are given for each intent. You can decide how you'd like to use them. My suggestions: use the given number as the amount of times you say your chant, the amount of crystals you place around the candle, or the number of ingredients you use in the spell. Otherwise, the number can be carved into the candle.

I've included a recommended lunar phase and solar phase for working with each intent. This adds an extra boost of power to your spell. However, you can disregard these recommendations if you do not want to wait to perform your spell. Days of the week are also listed. Likewise, they are just suggestions.

I have shared the planets that correspond to each intent. You can work their energy into your spells by carving the planetary symbol onto the candle or by including an extra candle in the spell, one that is dedicated to the specific planet.

Zodiac signs have been given for each intent. These can be used to symbolise a person, or you can wait until the moon is in that sign to perform your spell. Like all timing suggestions, this is optional.

Tarot cards that correspond with the energy of the spell are provided. Cards can be used as a focus for any kind of spell; they provide an image for you to draw upon to add energy to the working. Place a corresponding tarot or oracle card in front of or behind your candle spell. When the spell is finished, place the card on your altar until the spell has come to fruition.

Crystal suggestions have been given. I chose common and easily available crystals. A tumbled stone is fine; the crystals do not have to be big or expensive. Once the spell is finished, the crystals can be cleansed and used again.

For each intent, I have also included the element it corresponds with. You can use this as a base point for tying in other ingredients, or you can carve the element symbol into the candle.

Do not forget to check out the "extras" section for each spell. This section has additional items that can be added to your spell.

Finally, above all, please do not be limited by my lists. Trust your intuition when choosing items to use and how to work with them.

Template for Spell Work

This is a basic template for spell work. I've included it here to give you an idea of how to proceed with your spells. This is how *I* work—remember, this is just an outline. I recommend personalising your spells, but my suggestions will get you started.

Spell Template

1. Charge the candle, herbs, oils, and any extras with your intent.

2. Carve corresponding symbol(s) into your candle.

3. Dress the candle with oil. Roll the dressed candle in your chosen herbs or sprinkle them around the base of the candle. Set the candle in a safe holder.

4. Place your petition underneath or in front of the candle, if using. The petition can also be lit from the flame and placed in a fireproof dish to burn out.

5. If using, place a tarot or oracle card behind the candle and a crystal in front.

6. Light the candle, say your chant, and visualise your intent.

7. Allow the candle to burn out.

CHAPTER TEN

Spells for Growth and Abundance

Perhaps the most common type of spell work is money drawing. This is considered a prosperity spell, but the word *prosperity* also applies to fertility, success, and new beginnings. And, of course, we could all do with a bit of luck now and then! You might want to combine some of these intents to achieve your goal.

A few tips: Focus on what you need and how you can work to obtain it rather than just asking for wads of cash. And don't forget to give thanks for what you receive! Tap into your inspiration and creativity when creating your spell. Think outside of the box—you might be unexpectedly surprised.

Prosperity

Prosperity, abundance, wealth, and money spells all pretty much cover the same subject. Intents can range from needing some fast cash, to requiring a significant amount of money for an unexpected bill, to wanting a stable income for your business, to covering general living expenses.

With that being said, abundance and wealth also refer to things other than money. A wealthy or abundant life could mean a good and positive life. You may have an abundance/wealth of friends and loved ones. Do not limit prosperity spells—they can do more than manifest cash.

Options

Colour	Green, gold, purple, orange, brown
Carrier Oil	Almond, sesame, sunflower
Dressing Direction	Draw the oil towards you to coat the candle
Herb/Oil	Basil, bergamot (orange), cedar, chamomile, cloves, cumin, dandelion, frankincense, ginger, grass, honeysuckle, jasmine, mint, nutmeg, patchouli, pine, poppy, rose, sage, sesame, sunflower, tea leaves (black)
Symbol	Currency sign such as a dollar, pound, or euro; infinity
Rune	Fehu, Gebo, Wunjo, Jera, Dagaz, Othila
Ogham	Duir/Oak, Quert/Apple, Edhadh/Aspen, Onn/Gorse, Muinn/Bramble, Gort/Ivy
Petition	Write in green, purple, or gold ink Write petition on foreign currency note
Number	8
Lunar Phase	Waxing, first quarter, full
Solar Phase	Mid-morning
Day of the Week	Thursday for abundance, finances, prosperity, and wealth Sunday for prosperity, success, and wealth Wednesday for fortune Tuesday for success
Planet	Jupiter for abundance, prosperity, and wealth Venus for good fortune, money, and success Moon for manifesting and riches Sun for prosperity Mars for success

Options

Zodiac Sign	Taurus for prosperity
	Virgo for prosperity
	Cancer for abundance
	Leo for fast cash
Tarot Card	Wheel of Fortune, Ten of Pentacles, Knight of Pentacles, Page of Pentacles, the Empress, the Star, the World, Ace of Pentacles, Six of Pentacles, Nine of Pentacles, Ace of Cups
Crystal	Green aventurine, bloodstone, goldstone, moss agate, malachite, pyrite, sunstone, tiger's eye
Element	Earth

Chant Suggestion

Richness of oils and herbs so sweet
Bring [fast cash/prosperity/abundance] to me, and make it neat
Now come in and bring it to me
Candle magic, provide abundance to see

Extras

To boost your prosperity spells, you can use currency and/or food—two things most of us have on hand.

+ Coins are a good item to use in prosperity spells, as they literally represent money. I like to work with small silver coins because they bring in silver colour magic. Coins can be placed in front of a candle whilst working a spell; I recommend creating a circle of small coins around your candle. You could carve a slot and push a coin into the side of the candle; once the candle burns down and releases the coin, your spell is done. Alternatively, you could push a small coin into the base of your candle. Coins can be used as prosperity charms after a spell is finished; place the coin on your altar or in your purse.

+ Chocolate is a good representation of abundance and wealth. It can be incorporated by placing squares of chocolate in front of your candle.

+ Nuts bring positive magical energy in the form of abundance. They can be placed in front of your candle or arranged in a circle around it.

+ You could fold up currency notes and set them under the candle or in front of it, but be mindful that they could catch flame or be ruined by the wax.

New Beginnings

A new beginning spell can be worked for any number of outcomes. You might want to start a new venture or business. Perhaps you want to start living your life in a new way or change your path. Candle magic can give you an energetic kickstart as you begin your new journey. It can also be used to open up new avenues and provide you with opportunities you didn't even know existed. Beginnings come in many forms—you just need to be open to discovering them.

Options

Colour	Blue, green, white
Carrier Oil	Olive, sunflower, sesame
Dressing Direction	Dress the oil towards you to start new energy
Herb/Oil	Dandelion, geranium, hawthorn, lemon, lemon balm, oak, pine, rose, sage, sunflower; seeds of all kinds can be used
Symbol	Awen, circle, triskelion, arrow, waxing crescent
Rune	Eihwaz, Sowilo, Berkana, Inguz
Ogham	Beith/Birch, Idho/Yew
Petition	Write petition with green or blue ink Write petition on a sage leaf or large green leaf
Number	1, 5
Lunar Phase	New, waxing crescent

Options

Solar Phase	Sunrise, morning
Day of the Week	Monday for fertility or success, as it is the beginning of the workweek
	Tuesday for success
	Thursday for growth
	Friday for fertility
	Sunday for personal achievements and success
Planet	Venus for fertility and success
	Jupiter for growth and success
	Sun for fertility and growth
	Moon for birth and fertility
Zodiac Sign	Aries for new projects, skills, and opportunities
	Gemini for ideas and learning
	Leo for opportunities
	Sagittarius for learning, optimism, and new techniques
Tarot Card	The Fool, the Emperor, the World, the Chariot, the Hermit, Death, the Sun, Two of Pentacles, Ten of Swords, Ace of Wands, Knight of Wands, Four of Cups, Eight of Cups
Crystal	Malachite, moonstone, moss agate
Element	Earth, air

Chant Suggestion

Candle flame to bring a breakthrough
Open doorways for beginnings anew
Opportunities may now arise
Allowing me to grasp the prize

Extras

New beginnings always says "growth" to me, which brings spring to mind, when everything is fresh and new.

- Plant some seeds in a pot. Place the pot in front of your candle spell as you work, then move the pot to a windowsill or set it outside.
- Place five green leaves of any kind around your candle spell as decoration.
- White flowers can be arranged around your candle spell to symbolise a new start.
- Place your candle on a white mat or a piece of white paper to represent a blank canvas.
- Clear everything from your altar, cleanse the space, and lay a white altar cloth. Leave the altar empty for a few days to signify that you are open to opportunities and new beginnings.

Fertility

Fertility comes in many forms, the obvious one being starting a family, and candle magic can certainly help with that (from a magical perspective—you guys need to do the work!). But new additions don't only arrive in baby form. You could adopt a pet or make a new friend. Fertility also correlates with new beginnings, as you could be "birthing" a new job or business venture. Allow candle magic to expand your idea of fertility; this word has realms of possibilities.

Options

Colour	Green, brown, white
Carrier Oil	Olive, sunflower, sesame
Dressing Direction	Dress the oil towards you to bring in fertility
Herb/Oil	Fennel, geranium, hawthorn, mustard, oak, pine, poppy seeds, sunflower; seeds of all kinds
Symbol	Awen, circle, moon, triskelion
Rune	Fehu, Berkana, Inguz

Options

Ogham	Saille/Willow, Huathe/Hawthorn, Coll/Hazel, Ailm/Pine
Petition	Write petition in green ink Write petition on the back of a seed packet
Number	1, 2, 4, 5, 6
Lunar Phase	New, waxing crescent
Solar Phase	Sunrise, morning
Day of the Week	Monday for fertility Friday for fertility
Planet	Venus for fertility Moon for birth and fertility Sun for fertility
Zodiac Sign	Cancer for fertility Leo for fertility Virgo for fertility Aries for new projects and skills
Tarot Card	The Sun, the Fool, the Empress, Ten of Cups, Ace of Wands
Crystal	Moss agate, moonstone, pebble, hag stone, rose quartz
Element	Earth, water

Chant Suggestion

Candle magic, bring me the ability
To create and manifest fertility
Fresh and new ideas, full and free
Fertility fulfilled, now let me see

Extras

For fertility, think all things associated with spring. Eggs are a wonderful representation, as are hares and rabbits.

+ Crush eggshells and dress your candle with them.
+ Arrange eggs (or egg decorations) in a circle around your candle.
+ Set a ring of chocolate eggs around your candle spell.
+ Print off a photograph of a hare or rabbit and set it in front of your candle spell. The image can be kept on your altar to call in fertile energy.
+ Oats are symbolic of fertility. Crush them into a powder and roll your candle in them.

Success

Success comes in many forms and for a variety of reasons. Success can be financial, certainly, but it is not always about money. You might be looking for success in a business venture or a creative endeavour, or you may be after a successful outcome for a game or event you are competing in. Perhaps you want a meeting or event to go well. Work a little success candle magic to ensure everything goes smoothly.

Options

Colour	Orange, purple, gold
Carrier Oil	Olive, sesame, sunflower
Dressing Direction	Dress the candle by drawing the oil towards you
Herb/Oil	Bergamot (orange), cinnamon, cumin, ginger, holly, lemon, lemon balm, mustard, rowan, sage
Symbol	Sun, circle, smiley face, solar cross
Rune	Wunjo, Jera, Sowilo, Berkana, Ehwaz, Dagaz
Ogham	Luis/Rowan

Options

Petition	Write petition in gold ink
	If the spell is for business, write petition on a business card or flyer
Number	8
Lunar Phase	Waxing gibbous, full
Solar Phase	Morning, high noon
Day of the Week	Tuesday for success
	Sunday for success
Planet	Mars for success and victory
	Sun for success
	Venus for success and victory
	Saturn for business success
Zodiac Sign	Virgo for success
	Leo for success
Tarot Card	The Chariot, Wheel of Fortune, Justice, the Star, the Moon, the Sun, the World, Ace of Pentacles, Queen of Pentacles, King of Pentacles, Ace of Swords, Two of Swords, Six of Swords
Crystal	Agate, amber, amethyst, carnelian, citrine, goldstone, labradorite, lapis lazuli, malachite, pyrite, rose quartz, selenite, tiger's eye, unakite
Element	Fire, earth

Chant Suggestion

Power of candle, bring me success
A positive outcome with no stress
Element of fire and flame so strong
Bring me the success where I belong

Extras

You can add all sorts of things to your spell working, but they need to represent success to you. How do *you* quantify success?

- Place a certificate you have earnt in front of your candle spell to represent success.
- If money represents success to you, place a generous bank statement in front of your spell.
- Jewels or sparkly bling can also represent success. These can be placed in a circle around your candle spell.
- Place a circle of your business cards around your candle; eight of them would work well.

Luck

We could all use a bit of luck from time to time, and candle magic can bring it right to you. Luck can be linked to prosperity and success; they often complement each other very well. But luck can be more than that. You might need luck for a job interview or a competitive event. You may want to add a bit of luck to your love life. Of course, you could also work a luck spell to win the lottery, because you never know…

Options

Colour	Green, gold, yellow
Carrier Oil	Olive, sunflower, almond
Dressing Direction	Dress the candle towards you to bring luck in
Herb/Oil	Clover, heather, holly, marigold, nutmeg, oak, poppy, rose, star anise, sunflower
Symbol	Four-leaf clover, horseshoe
Rune	Fehu, Uruz, Thurisaz, Gebo, Pertho, Berkana
Ogham	Duir/Oak, Tinne/Holly, Coll/Hazel, Ur/Heather

Options

Petition	Write petition in gold or green ink
	Write petition on an old lottery ticket
Number	3, 5, 6
Lunar Phase	First quarter, waxing gibbous, full
Solar Phase	Morning, high noon
Day of the Week	Thursday for luck
	Wednesday for luck and cunning
	Sunday for success and victory
Planet	Jupiter for luck and success
Zodiac Sign	Pisces for luck
Tarot Card	The World, the Star, Wheel of Fortune
Crystal	Amethyst, carnelian, goldstone, green aventurine, labradorite, lapis lazuli, pyrite, rose quartz, smoky quartz, sunstone, tiger's eye, turquoise
Element	Earth

Chant Suggestion

Magic of the candle here and now
Bring me luck and show me how
Upon me luck now bestow
As above and so below!

Extras

Whilst I do believe we create our own destiny (and even our own positive energy), we all need a bit of luck on occasion. Heather and the four-leaf clover have always been symbols of luck for me. What about you?

- Cut out pictures of four-leaf clovers and spread them around your candle spell.

- Horseshoes are said to be lucky. If you have one, set it in front of your candle spell.
- Rainbows bring luck, particularly when they have a pot of gold at the end. Put a picture or image of a rainbow on your altar.
- Circle your candle spell with gold coins to bring in good luck.

Inspiration and Creativity

If your creative flow has slowed way down or inspiration has left the building, then candle magic can help relight the flame, literally! Candle magic brings in the element of fire, which is jam-packed with inspiration, motivation, and energy. Use magic to fill your mind with ideas, prompts, and projects that will get you going.

Options

Colour	Orange, yellow, red, blue, green, purple, violet
Carrier Oil	Almond, olive
Dressing Direction	Dress the candle towards you to bring creativity
Herb/Oil	Bay, chillies, rowan, vanilla
Symbol	Awen
Rune	Uruz, Kenaz, Pertho, Inguz, Ansuz, Othila
Ogham	Beith/Birch, Luis/Rowan, Fearn/Alder, Tinne/Holly, Muinn/Bramble, Saille/Willow, Coll/Hazel
Petition	Write petition in multicoloured ink Write petition on patterned paper Write petition on a printed-out image of art
Number	3, 4
Lunar Phase	New, waxing crescent, first quarter
Solar Phase	Sunrise, the morning
Day of the Week	Wednesday for creativity Sunday for inspiration

Options

Planet	Sun for creativity and inspiration
	Venus for creativity and inspiration
Zodiac Sign	Aries for creativity
	Taurus for creativity
	Leo for creativity
	Aquarius for creativity and inspiration
	Pisces for creativity
Tarot Card	The Magician, the Moon, the Star
Crystal	Amethyst, bloodstone, blue lace agate, carnelian, citrine, goldstone, green aventurine, labradorite, malachite, moss agate, orange calcite, pyrite, rose quartz, smoky quartz, sunstone, tiger's eye, tourmaline
Element	Fire

Chant Suggestion

Fire and passion bring to me
The flame of brilliant creativity
Magic inspire me, fill my heart
To create, and inspiration impart

Extras

Whether or not you share your art with others, we are all artists.

+ Include an image of your favourite artwork in front of your candle spell.
+ Lay your creativity tools around the candle, such as pens, paintbrushes, etc.
+ Dress your altar with flowers, sparkles, and all kinds of over-the-top decorations.

CHAPTER ELEVEN

Spells for Healing and Insight

Healing comes in many forms and covers a wide variety of issues, whether they are physical, mental, or spiritual. Some healing requires change and transformation to take place before it can begin. Often, healing involves making decisions and allowing things to evolve. But don't just think of healing as improving physical health or curing an illness—there are many layers and dimensions to it.

You can bring about healing by determining the root cause of an issue and then taking steps to resolve it. Insight and clarity are also beneficial goals, and sometimes very necessary ones. Gaining a new perspective can change the desired outcome of a situation.

Healing

There is no better way to work healing magic than with a candle spell. You can request health for yourself or a loved one, but keep in mind that not everyone wants healing sent to them, and the Universe may have other ideas as well.

We all have free will, so it is advisable to request permission before sending healing to another person; not doing so is an ethical issue. If you are unable to contact them but still wish to send healing, try sending healing out to the Universe. Ask the Universe to direct it to those that want it.

Options

Colour	Blue, green, pink, red
Carrier Oil	Olive, sesame
Dressing Direction	Dress towards you to bring in healing or good health
Herb/Oil	Bay, blackthorn, cinnamon, coriander, fennel, ginger, juniper, lemon balm, lungwort, marjoram, mint, myrrh, nettle, oak, pine, rose, rosemary, rowan, thyme
Symbol	Circle, heart
Rune	Uruz, Sowilo
Ogham	Luis/Rowan, Saille/Willow, Nuinn/Ash, Huathe/Hawthorn, Duir/Oak, Quert/Apple, Muinn/Bramble, Gort/Ivy, Ngeadal/Broom, Ailm/Pine
Petition	Write petition in blue or green ink Use an old prescription as petition paper Write petition on the back of a photograph of the person that needs healing
Number	3, 6
Lunar Phase	Waxing or full to bring healing or good health Waning moon to dispel illness
Solar Phase	Sunrise, morning, or high noon to bring good health Afternoon or sunset to dispel illness
Day of the Week	Monday for healing Thursday for healing and good health
Planet	Jupiter for healing and health Mercury for healing Moon for health and healing Saturn for healing

Options

Zodiac Sign	Scorpio for healing Virgo for healing and health Gemini for healing
Tarot Card	Strength, the World, the Magician, the Sun, the Star, the Empress, the Chariot, Judgement, Three of Cups
Crystal	Agate, amber, bloodstone, celestite, citrine, fluorite, green aventurine, hematite, jasper, labradorite, malachite, moonstone, quartz, rose quartz, selenite, sunstone, tiger's eye
Element	Water

Chant Suggestion

Candle power to bring good health and to heal
Positive energy to improve how we feel
Negative energy and illness remove
Healing and health now we approve

Extras

No matter how well we look after our health, we all need a bit of healing sometimes. Or perhaps another needs healing. Regardless, the energy of a candle spell can really help.

+ Place a photograph of the person who needs healing under the candle.
+ If you take medication of any kind, it can be placed around the candle or in front of it to represent healing.
+ When I think of healing, I think of the words *soothing* and *calming*. To signify this, add a dab of moisturiser or balm to the corners of your petition.
+ Stand a pot of vitamins or herbal supplements in front of your candle, or take some tablets out and arrange them in a circle around your candle.

Decisions and Direction

Life often throws us into situations that do not have an obvious way out or through. Not knowing how to move forward can be really frustrating. Spell work can shed light on options that you haven't considered. Alternatively, you may be faced with too many options or be asked to make an impossible choice. This can be really confusing and overwhelming. Either way, candle magic can help you find some definite direction.

Options

Colour	Blue, yellow, brown, red, green, white
Carrier Oil	Almond, sesame, sunflower
Dressing Direction	Dress the candle towards you to bring clarity and direction
Herb/Oil	Cardamom, clove, coffee, juniper, lavender, lemon, mustard
Symbol	Cross, arrow
Rune	Thurisaz, Raidho, Naudhiz, Sowilo, Ansuz, Dagaz
Ogham	Fearn/Alder, Quert/Apple, Ailm/Pine, Onn/Gorse
Petition	Write petition in blue, red, or green ink Write petition on a map, printed or from an old map book Draw a cross with the four directions; write petition on top
Number	2, 4
Lunar Phase	Third quarter, waxing gibbous
Solar Phase	Sunrise, mid-afternoon
Day of the Week	Monday for clarity
Planet	Sun for clarity
Zodiac Sign	Libra for decisions

Options

Tarot Card	Justice, the Hermit, the Star, the Lovers
Crystal	Carnelian, fluorite, goldstone, green aventurine, hematite, labradorite, lapis lazuli, pyrite, quartz, selenite, smoky quartz, sunstone, unakite
Element	Air

Chant Suggestion

Candle magic, please show me how
To make the decision, which direction now
Help to show me the way
In which direction my destiny might lay

Extras

If you were seeking direction in the physical world, what would you turn to? Those same items can be used in spell work.

+ Place a compass in front of your candle spell.
+ Lay an old map underneath your candle spell.

Peace and Harmony

Wherever we are in the world, it would be nice to be in a peaceful and harmonious situation, but it doesn't always work that way. You can work a spell for peace and harmony in a relationship or at home after a confrontation or disagreement. You could even work a spell for world peace, which is always a good intent. Use candle magic in any situation to bring about calm, positive, peaceful vibes.

Options

Colour	Blue, white
Carrier Oil	Olive, coconut

Options

Dressing Direction	Dress the candle towards you to bring in peace and harmony
Herb/Oil	Basil, coriander, cumin, lavender, poppy, thyme, yarrow
Symbol	Circle, smiley face, triquetra, triskelion, cross
Rune	Jera, Inguz, Othila, Fehu, Uruz, Wunjo
Ogham	Nuinn/Ash, Tinne/Holly, Quert/Apple, Gort/Ivy, Ngeadal/Broom
Petition	Use white paper and write with blue ink
Number	2
Lunar Phase	New, dark
Solar Phase	Sunrise, sunset
Day of the Week	Monday for peace Friday for harmony
Planet	Venus for harmony and peace Sun for harmony and peace Jupiter for peace
Zodiac Sign	Libra for harmony and peace
Tarot Card	The Star, Five of Cups, the Hermit, Temperance
Crystal	Agate, amethyst, carnelian, celestine, fluorite, green aventurine, jasper, lapis lazuli, malachite, moonstone, orange calcite, rose quartz, sodalite, sunstone, tourmaline, turquoise, unakite
Element	Earth, water

Chant Suggestion

Candle magic, now sweep in
Clear out the negative for a win

Chaotic vibes will now decrease
Gentle energy that brings in peace

Extras

A wide variety of items can be used for peaceful intent.

+ The words *peace* and *harmony* bring to mind cool colours such as white and pale blue. Use colour magic to set the scene. Dress your altar in a plain white cloth. Bring in a vase of white flowers. Tie your petition or candle with blue ribbon.

+ Print an image of a dove and set it in front of your candle spell. The dove symbolises peace.

+ Play gentle, soulful music to enhance peaceful energy.

+ Nature brings harmony and peace, so decorate your altar with greenery. You could also place images of forests and other green spaces around your candle spell.

+ Butter corresponds with peace. Dress your candle with butter instead of oil.

Clarity, Insight, and Truth

If you need insight or clarity on a situation, then candle magic can help. Spell workings can also be done to find the truth in a situation. Or perhaps you need to look at things from a different point of view. It is really easy to find yourself in a situation where you cannot see the wood for the trees, and a new perspective can clear things up. The fire from a candle spell burns through all the murkiness and brings clarity and truth.

Options

Colour	White, black, blue, yellow
Carrier Oil	Almond, sesame, sunflower
Dressing Direction	Dress the candle towards you to bring clarity and insight, or away from you to uncover the truth

Options

Herb/Oil	Cardamom, clove, coffee, juniper, lavender, mustard, pine, rosemary, sunflower
Symbol	Awen, triquetra, cross, eye, keyhole
Rune	Dagaz, Ansuz, Mannaz, Teiwaz
Ogham	Ailm/Pine, Huathe/Hawthorn, Coll/Hazel, Edhadh/Aspen, Muinn/Bramble
Petition	Write petition in black or blue ink Write petition on a piece of reflective foil Draw an eye and write petition on top
Number	2, 7, 9
Lunar Phase	Dark, full, first quarter, waxing gibbous
Solar Phase	Sunrise, high noon, morning
Day of the Week	Monday for clarity and intuition
Planet	Mercury for insight and understanding Sun for clarity and truth
Zodiac Sign	Aquarius for clarity and intuition Scorpio for insight and revealing secrets Libra for insight Pisces for intuition
Tarot Card	The High Priestess, the Lovers, Justice, the Tower, the Moon, Ace of Swords, Knight of Wands, Seven of Cups, Queen of Cups
Crystal	Agate, amber, amethyst, bloodstone, celestite, citrine, goldstone, labradorite, lapis lazuli, malachite, moonstone, orange calcite, pyrite, quartz, selenite, smoky quartz, sunstone, tiger's eye, turquoise
Element	Air

Chant Suggestion

Candle magic, show to me the truth
Uncover the secrets like a sleuth
Reveal to me that which is unseen
Lay out the facts perfectly clean

Extras

Insight can be found by looking at things differently. Use reflective surfaces to reveal the truth.

* Set your candle spell on a mirrored surface to help reveal the truth.
* Place images of birds on your altar to gain a different perspective of the situation.
* Situate a small mirror behind your candle so it reflects the flame.
* Put a pair of glasses, a magnifying glass, or binoculars in front of your candle to enhance insight.
* Draw an eye on a sheet of paper and place it under your candle.

Change and Transformation

One certainty in life is that things change. Sometimes those changes are difficult to deal with. Alternatively, you might be craving change and transformation in your life. Perhaps you are eager to change the way you handle things. Nevertheless, the road to change can be a bumpy one, so help it go smoothly with a little bit of candle magic. Magic can usher in change and transformation, and it can help us deal with any emotions or issues that arise during periods of transition.

Options

Colour	Blue, orange
Carrier Oil	Sunflower, sesame, olive
Dressing Direction	Dress the candle towards you to bring in change
Herb/Oil	Benzoin, chamomile, cinnamon, lungwort, mint, patchouli, poppy

Options

Symbol	Wheel, sun, moon, solar cross, arrow, cross
Rune	Dagaz, Raidho, Eihwaz, Ehwaz
Ogham	Beith/Birch, Tinne/Holly, Ruis/Elder
Petition	Write petition in blue ink
Number	5, 9
Lunar Phase	New, waxing crescent, first quarter, full
Solar Phase	Sunrise, morning, high noon
Day of the Week	Wednesday for changes, guidance, and luck Tuesday for challenges, confidence, and courage
Planet	Moon for changes and transformation Sun for transformation Mars for courage, independence, and problem-solving
Zodiac Sign	Gemini for transformation and communication Libra for compromise and decisions
Tarot Card	Wheel of Fortune, the Magician, the Hanged Man, Death, the Tower, Judgement, the World, Knight of Swords, Eight of Wands
Crystal	Amethyst, citrine, labradorite, malachite, orange calcite, tourmaline, unakite
Element	Air, fire

Chant Suggestion

Candle energy, support me in transition
Changes I accept with submission
Enable me to go with the flow
Trust in the best outcome I know

Extras

Change is really a journey. Some journeys are long, some are short, and some of them are really bumpy.

* Use two candles, one to represent "before" and another "after." Light the "before" candle, then light the "after" candle from it.

* Use three candles to represent the past, the present, and the future. Light the past candle, then light the present candle from it. Light the future candle from the present candle.

* Find or draw an image that represents where you are now, and another that represents where you want to be. Place both on your altar.

* Set a photograph or image of your goal under the candle.

* Lay an old map underneath your candle spell to represent the journey.

Balance

Finding balance in life seems to be an eternal struggle. We're constantly juggling family, work, socialising, self-care, caring for others, and all the day-to-day tasks that have to be done. Sure, we all want to find the perfect balance, but it can be difficult to determine which small changes could bring about that balance. Candle magic can help you find balance in your everyday life (and also show you how to maintain it).

Options

Colour	Blue, brown, green
Carrier Oil	Sesame, sunflower
Dressing Direction	Dress the candle towards you to bring about balance
	Dress the upper half of the candle away from you to release and the lower half towards you to bring in balance
	Using two candles, dress one away from you to release and one towards you to bring in balance

Options

Herb/Oil	Chamomile, holly, honeysuckle, patchouli, witch hazel
Symbol	Scales, circle, triquetra, solar cross, cross
Rune	Mannaz, Dagaz, Othila
Ogham	Saille/Willow, Nuinn/Ash
Petition	Use two separate petitions, one to represent what you want to release and one for what you would like to bring in
Number	2
Lunar Phase	Full
Solar Phase	High noon
Day of the Week	Wednesday for change Tuesday for challenges, courage, and success
Planet	Venus for emotions, happiness, and harmony Mercury for communication and understanding
Zodiac Sign	Libra for balance and harmony
Tarot Card	The Lovers, Justice, Temperance, Two of Swords, Four of Wands, Two of Cups
Crystal	Agate, amber, fluorite, green aventurine, hematite, jasper, moonstone, quartz, rose quartz, selenite, sunstone, tiger's eye, tourmaline, turquoise
Element	All four together: earth, air, fire, and water

Chant Suggestion

Balance is the goal I seek
Hear me now, the truth I speak
Release that which I no longer need
Bring in balance with great speed

Extras

In spell work and on your altar, try to use even numbers and colours that complement each other.

- Use two candles to represent balance. I like to work with black and white or silver and gold.
- Add weights from a set of scales to your altar, or set them in front of your candle spell.
- Lay out two altar cloths, one dark and one light to represent balance.
- Include images of both the sun and the moon to represent balance.
- Use the yin-yang symbol in your candle spell.
- Oysters represent balance. If you have some empty shells, use them as decoration.

CHAPTER TWELVE

Spells for Protection

Protection can be easily achieved using candle magic, whether in the form of physical, mental, or emotional protection. One way to protect yourself is by grounding, particularly after any kind of energy work. Binding is an area of spell work that I don't use very often, but it is a successful way to protect yourself or your family without causing harm.

I've also included spells for psychic skills in this chapter, as these skills work nicely alongside protection, which is wise to have in place when doing any psychic work. Candle magic increases and enhances psychic skills and is a very useful conduit for all sorts of spirit world contact and connection.

Protection

Protection spells are a wise precaution for most magical workers, but they can also be used to protect children at school or when out and about. Protection can be physical (for example, a spell to keep you safe while driving) or even psychic (protection for when you are working with spirit, or when you need to shield yourself from the energy of others). Don't forget that items used in protection spells can be carried with you after the magic has been worked to carry the protective energy forward.

Options

Colour	Black, white, blue (for spiritual protection), brown, red, silver
Carrier Oil	Coconut, olive, sesame
Dressing Direction	Dress the oil towards you to bring in protection or away from you to dispel negative energy
Herb/Oil	Basil, bay, benzoin, black pepper, black thorn, cardamom, chillies, cinnamon, clove, copal, cumin, dragon's blood, ginger, hawthorn, lavender, lemon, mint, mustard, nutmeg, patchouli, pine, rose, rosemary, sage, salt, star anise, witch hazel, yarrow
Symbol	Circle, X, horseshoe, eye, wheel, key
Rune	Thurisaz, Eihwaz, Algiz, Teiwaz
Ogham	Beith/Birch, Luis/Rowan, Fearn/Alder, Saille/Willow, Nuinn/Ash, Huathe/Hawthorn, Duir/Oak, Tinne/Holly, Coll/Hazel, Muinn/Bramble, Gort/Ivy, Straif/Blackthorn, Edhadh/Aspen
Petition	Write your petition with black ink or on black paper
Number	2, 6
Lunar Phase	New, waxing, full
Solar Phase	Mid-morning, high noon
Day of the Week	Monday, Tuesday, Thursday, Saturday
Planet	Jupiter for protection Moon for protection
Zodiac Sign	Aries for protection Pisces for banishing
Tarot Card	The Empress, the Emperor

Options

Crystal	Agate, amethyst, bloodstone, carnelian, hematite, labradorite, obsidian, pebble, pyrite, quartz, selenite, sunstone, tiger's eye, tourmaline, turquoise
Element	Fire

Chant Suggestion

Candle magic, flame so bright
Bring to me every day and night
The safety and security of protection
Dispel negative energy off in another direction

Extras

Nails and thorns are very symbolic of protection and can be used in candle magic. If you can get ahold of old nails—or, even better, coffin nails—that is preferred. Thorns of all kinds also bring protection, particularly those of the blackthorn or rose.

+ Push a thorn or nail into your candle. When the wax melts and the thorn or nail falls out, the spell is done.
+ Place six nails or thorns around the base of your candle. Once the spell is done, the nails or thorns are charged with protective energy and can be carried with you or placed on your altar.
+ Collect any herbs or dried plant matter used in your spell work and pop them into a pouch. Carry the pouch with you for continued protection.

Psychic and Spirit Work

Candle spells can boost your psychic abilities and/or build a connection to the Otherworld and realms of the spirit. The combination of elements within candle magic really creates a strong, focused, direct line to spirit. The flame of a candle serves as a focal point to help you hone and tune in to your psychic abilities. You have the power within, and candle magic can help you release it!

Options

Colour	White, black, blue, purple, silver, violet
Carrier Oil	Almond, olive
Dressing Direction	Dress the candle towards you to activate your skills
Herb/Oil	Bay, cinnamon, dandelion, grass, honeysuckle, juniper, marigold, rose, rowan, sage, star anise, thyme, yarrow
Symbol	Pentagram, moon, triquetra, spiral, eye, key
Rune	Pertho, Laguz
Ogham	Luis/Rowan, Straif/Blackthorn
Petition	Write petition in purple ink Draw an eye and write petition on it
Number	3, 5, 7, 8, 9
Lunar Phase	Dark, full
Solar Phase	High noon, sunrise, sunset
Day of the Week	Monday for psychic abilities, dreams, and intuition Saturday for spirituality
Planet	Moon for divination, mysteries, and spirituality Jupiter for psychic skills and spirituality Mercury for divination and dream work
Zodiac Sign	Cancer for psychic abilities Scorpio for psychic development Pisces for psychic abilities
Tarot Card	The High Priestess, the Devil, the Moon
Crystal	Amber, citrine, green aventurine, labradorite, malachite, moonstone, pyrite, quartz, selenite, sodalite, tiger's eye, turquoise for psychic abilities Black obsidian, celestite, garnet, quartz, selenite for spirit work
Element	Air

Chant Suggestion

Candle magic, light my psychic eye
Allow my insight skills to fly
Truth and clarity, show me how
Open the third eye on my brow

Extras

Honing your psychic skills takes practice. The more you work at it, the better you will become. Candle magic provides a wonderful atmosphere to work in.

+ Place your divination tool(s) in front of a candle as you work the spell. The energy from the candle will charge them.
+ Choose a special crystal just for psychic work. This can be charged as you work your candle spell, then brought out when you do any psychic or spirit work.

Grounding

Ever feel like you are floating about with your head in the clouds, and your thoughts all scattered? You could definitely benefit from some grounding. Instant grounding can be effected by doing a short mental exercise, but long-term, it can be of benefit to work a grounding spell, particularly if you feel completely out of tune with the world, your life, and everyone around you. Get those feet back firmly on the ground and connect with Mother Earth.

Options

Colour	Brown, green
Carrier Oil	Sesame
Dressing Direction	Dress the candle drawing the oil towards you
Herb/Oil	Grass, patchouli, salt, tree bark
Symbol	Earth triangle, tree
Rune	Isa, Inguz, Othila
Ogham	Duir/Oak, Muinn/Bramble, Idho/Yew

Options

Petition	Write in brown or green ink Use brown or handcrafted paper Write petition on a large leaf Write petition on a piece of tree bark
Number	1
Lunar Phase	Waning gibbous, third quarter, waning crescent, dark
Solar Phase	Sunset
Day of the Week	Thursday for earth magic and grounding
Planet	Saturn for home, safety, and structure
Zodiac Sign	Sagittarius for grounding Taurus for connection, practical matters, and stability
Tarot Card	Temperance, Strength, Judgement
Crystal	Amethyst, carnelian, fluorite, hematite, jasper, labradorite, obsidian, pyrite, rose quartz, smoky quartz, tiger's eye, tourmaline
Element	Earth

Chant Suggestion

Power of candle and magic found
Bring me balance and help me ground
Centre and focus, my feet on the floor
Floating away will be no more

Extras

The best way to call in grounding energy is by using the ingredients Mother Earth naturally provides.

+ Stand your candle in a dish of soil to represent the earth and a grounding connection.
+ Place a dish of soil or salt in front of your candle spell.

• Place an image of a tree in front of your spell. Pay attention to the roots belowground, holding the tree firmly in place.

Binding

Once in a while, we encounter a situation, issue, or person so destructive that we need to work some magic to defend and protect ourselves. This is a situation where I work a binding. Binding does not harm anyone. Rather, it stops a person or a situation from causing further harm to you. We all have a right to protect and defend ourselves, and binding is incredibly useful for just that.

Options

Colour	Burgundy, red, black
Carrier Oil	Sesame
Dressing Direction	Dress the candle in a spiral, echoing the binding action of the spell
Herb/Oil	Bergamot (orange), blackthorn, dragon's blood, rowan, yarrow
Symbol	Pentagram, X, period/full stop
Rune	Isa
Ogham	Gort/Ivy
Petition	Write petition in red or black ink Write on a photograph of the person you are binding
Number	1, 9
Lunar Phase	Dark
Solar Phase	High noon, sunset
Day of the Week	Saturday for binding and justice
Planet	Saturn for binding, boundaries, and power Mars for aggression, assertion, and defence
Zodiac Sign	Scorpio for banishing and personal power Pisces for action and banishing

Options

Tarot Card	Temperance, Two of Swords, Eight of Swords, the Hanged Man
Crystal	Banded agate, obsidian, tiger's eye
Element	Fire

Chant Suggestion

To protect and defend, this [person/situation] I bind
Sorrow, hurt, and pain I leave behind
No harm to come
This binding is done

Extras

Binding does what it says: it binds someone or something. That action can be echoed in the items you use for the spell.

- If binding a person, tie a photograph of them to your candle using twine or string. (Make sure the fabric you use will burn safely.)
- Poppets can be used to represent someone. Bind the dedicated poppet with string, twine, or even sticky tape.
- I like to cast a circle of salt before I work a binding spell, just to bring in some personal protection.
- Instead of using oil to dress your candle, you can use honey, maple syrup, or syrup of any kind. The stickiness of the ingredient helps build the binding energy.

CHAPTER THIRTEEN

Spells for Relationships and Positive Emotions

Working magic for relationships and love is tricky; do bear in mind the notion of free will when using magic of this type. Sometimes things just aren't meant to be and shouldn't be interfered with.

I have included spells for improved communication in this chapter as well, because how often have you had communication issues within a relationship? Candle magic can help you speak freely—be prepared for a new, confident, outspoken you! Confidence, courage, and strength can all be increased via candle magic, as can emotions such as happiness. We all need a bit of a boost on occasion, and magic can really help.

Love

Love spells are usually worked for one of two reasons: to draw in love, often in the form of a life partner, or for self-love (and we could all do with a bit more of that!). Love spells can be extremely successful, but I recommend keeping the wording very loose. Whilst I typically advocate being extremely specific with your words, will, and intent, this does not apply to love spells. Don't make a list of requirements, and be careful what you wish for—it may not be what you actually want. For instance, asking for someone with a sense of humour may bring in a person that constantly jokes around, which could be very annoying.

I never advise directing a love spell at a particular person. Not only does it go against their free will, it might have a disastrous end result. The person you believe is right for you may not actually be. And anyway, why would you want to be with someone who is only there because they were brought to you via magical means? Keep your love requests open-ended. Ask that the Universe/Divine/Deity send someone to you that is your perfect match.

Options

Colour	Red, pink
Carrier Oil	Almond, olive
Dressing Direction	Dress the candle towards you to bring love in
Herb/Oil	Basil, benzoin, cardamom, chamomile, cinnamon, cocoa, copal, cumin, daisy, geranium, ginger, hawthorn, jasmine, lavender, lemon balm, rose, rosemary, thyme, vanilla, yarrow
Symbol	Heart, infinity
Rune	Gebo, Wunjo
Ogham	Saille/Willow, Quert/Apple, Ur/Heather
Petition	Write petition with red or pink ink Write petition on flowery or heart-shaped paper Write petition on large rose petals or rose leaves
Number	2, 6
Lunar Phase	New, waxing, full
Solar Phase	Sunrise, mid-morning, high noon
Day of the Week	Friday for love, passion, relationships, romance, and attraction
Planet	Venus for love, passion, and attraction Jupiter for love Sun for love, friendship, and harmony

Options

Zodiac Sign	Taurus for love
	Libra for love and friendship
	Cancer for romance
Tarot Card	The Lovers, Knight of Cups, the Star, Two of Cups, Ace of Cups, Four of Wands
Crystal	Carnelian, lapis lazuli, malachite, moonstone, rose quartz, selenite, sodalite, sunstone, turquoise, unakite
Element	Water

Chant Suggestion

Warmth and magic of the candle flame
Bring my true love to me, I know not the name
Universe, in you I place my trust
Real love to me, more than lust

Extras

Charms, candy, and flowers can be used in love magic spells to great effect.

+ Place two or six heart-shaped candy sweets around the base of your candle.

+ Push a heart-shaped charm into the side of your candle or place it at the base. Once the spell is worked, this charm can be carried with you.

+ Roses have long symbolised love. Place a vase of roses beside your candle spell.

+ Sprinkle red or pink rose petals all around your sacred space where you are working the spell.

+ Place a heart-shaped crystal at the base of your candle spell. Once the spell is worked, this can be carried with you.

Gratitude

We are so used to asking for things that we sometimes forget to be thankful for what we have. Every so often, I work a gratitude spell as a way of saying thanks to the Universe, the Divine, and Mother Earth for all the good things in my life.

Gratitude spells can be worked individually, but they are also good to work with a group. You don't even need to be in the same place—group gratitude spells can be worked across the globe by many people at the same time. Set a date and time and share the spell instructions. Then everyone can work the spell together from different locations, sending the gratitude energy into the Universe.

Options

Colour	White, yellow, brown, pink
Carrier Oil	Almond, olive, sesame, sunflower
Dressing Direction	Draw the oil towards you, as you are bringing in the thanks
Herb/Oil	Basil, daisy, hawthorn, lavender, lemon, marigold, marjoram, sunflower, yarrow
Symbol	Smiley face
Rune	Uruz
Ogham	Gort/Ivy, Onn/Gorse
Petition	Write petition in pink or brown ink Just write the words *thank you* on petition
Number	3, 4, 5, 6, 8
Lunar Phase	Full
Solar Phase	High noon
Day of the Week	Any day of the week

Options

Planet	Moon for gratitude
	Jupiter for abundance and good fortune
	Mercury for understanding
	Sun for friendships and love
	Venus for happiness and harmony
Zodiac Sign	Taurus for comfort
	Cancer for abundance and nurturing
	Virgo for harvest and reaping rewards
Tarot Card	Ten of Pentacles, Nine of Cups, Six of Pentacles, the Sun, Six of Wands, Four of Swords, the Empress, Strength, Ace of Cups
Crystal	Agate, amethyst, citrine, fluorite, green aventurine, moonstone, sunstone
Element	Earth

Chant Suggestion

Sending out my love and gratitude
For all I have in life, love, health, and food
With my thanks, I send it out
I am grateful, there is no doubt

Extras

I recommend using personal items in your gratitude spells for an extra-strong connection.

+ If there is something you are particularly grateful for, use something to represent it. For example, a photograph of the holiday you had, or a family photo placed in front of your candle spell.
+ Food works well in gratitude spells. Place some chocolate, fruit, or vegetables in a display around your candle.

- Wine, beer, or mead is perfect for representing thanks. Place a glass in front of your candle spell. When the spell is finished, take a sip of the drink and pour some outside onto the land as an offering.

- Write a list of everything you are thankful for. Even the smallest things can be included. Fold the list up and place it under or in front of your candle. After the spell is finished, keep it on your altar as a reminder.

Confidence and Courage

We all need some extra self-confidence from time to time. Each of us has inner confidence and courage, but sometimes it needs a bit of a prompt. This type of spell can be worked as a general nudge, but it also works before a specific event or situation. Perhaps you have a big meeting with your boss coming up, or you have to speak in front of an audience for some reason. Candle magic can give you the extra boost of confidence and courage that you need.

Options

Colour	Orange, yellow, brown, red
Carrier Oil	Sunflower, olive, sesame
Dressing Direction	Dress the oil towards you to bring in confidence and courage
Herb/Oil	Bay, benzoin, black pepper, daisy, fennel, lavender, myrrh, oak, sesame, sunflower, tea (black), thyme, yarrow
Symbol	Awen, circle, pentagram, sun, arrow, horns
Rune	Fehu, Sowilo, Teiwaz, Inguz for confidence Uruz, Teiwaz for courage
Ogham	Fearn/Alder for confidence Fearn/Alder, Nuinn/Ash, Duir/Oak for courage
Petition	Write petition in brown or red ink
Number	1, 2, 4, 5, 6, 8

Options

Lunar Phase	Full, waxing
Solar Phase	Sunrise, morning, high noon
Day of the Week	Tuesday for confidence, courage, and challenge Sunday for personal achievements Thursday for strength
Planet	Mars for courage, independence, and strength Sun for confidence
Zodiac Sign	Taurus for confidence Leo for confidence and courage Aries for courage and bravery
Tarot Card	The Emperor, the Chariot for confidence The Star, Strength, the Chariot, the Fool, Ace of Swords, Knight of Swords, Seven of Wands, Nine of Wands for courage
Crystal	Carnelian, citrine, fluorite, goldstone, jasper, labra- dorite, lapis lazuli, moonstone, orange calcite, pyrite, sodalite, tiger's eye, unakite
Element	Earth, fire

Chant Suggestion

Candle magic, flame burning tall and strong
Bring courage and confidence to me all day long
Fill me with the power of a lion's roar
Confidence, courage, and much more

Extras

Colour magic plays a big part in feeling confident and courageous. It might be that when you wear a particular colour, you feel confident in it. Bright colours bring me courage and confidence, but you may prefer darker ones—it is a personal thing.

- Dress your altar with a brightly coloured cloth.
- Place a vase of brightly coloured flowers on your altar, beside your spell.
- Wear something that makes you feel fabulous whilst you are working your spell.
- Charge a piece of jewellery, a badge, or a lapel pin as you work your spell. Place it in front of the candle. Once the spell is finished, wear the item to bring in confidence and courage.

Strength

We all need a boost of strength on occasion. Maybe you need some strength to deal with a personal issue. Perhaps you just need to feel strong in general. I am not talking physical strength, although candle magic can certainly help with that too—strength spells give you the mental and/or spiritual stamina to get through a challenging situation. You may feel the need for a strength spell during a particularly hard day (or week, or month, or year) or when faced with a difficult person or issue.

Options

Colour	White, black, yellow, red
Carrier Oil	Sesame, sunflower
Dressing Direction	Dress the candle towards you to bring in strength
Herb/Oil	Bay, black pepper, daisy, lavender, oak, sesame, sunflower, tea
Symbol	Pentacle
Rune	Uruz, Thurisaz, Eihwaz, Sowilo, Teiwaz, Ehuwaz, Laguz
Ogham	Duir/Oak, Gort/Ivy, Ngeadal/Broom
Petition	Write petition in black or red ink Print an image of the Strength tarot card and write petition on it

Options

Number	4
Lunar Phase	Full moon, new moon, waxing moon
Solar Phase	Sunrise, morning, high noon
Day of the Week	Tuesday for strength, confidence, and courage Thursday for strength
Planet	Mars for strength
Zodiac Sign	Aries for strength Leo for strength
Tarot Card	Strength, Six of Wands, the Emperor, the Star, the Lovers, Nine of Wands, Seven of Wands, Six of Swords, any of the Kings
Crystal	Agate, bloodstone, hematite, labradorite, malachite, obsidian, pyrite, quartz, sunstone, tiger's eye, unakite
Element	Earth, fire

Chant Suggestion

Candle magic, I ask of thee
Give me strength; send it to me
Power and courage to make me strong
To help me move my life along

Extras

The following add-ons work well whether you are doing this spell for physical, mental, emotional, or spiritual strength.

- Place a photograph of a person who you feel carries strength behind your candle.
- Place weights from a set of scales around your spell to symbolise strength.
- Circle your spell with elastic or rubber bands to show the strength of bending without breaking.

Happiness

Everyone deserves a little happiness in life—more than a little! Candle magic can easily bring about happiness, joy, and harmony. Work this spell to bring about a much happier life for yourself, your friends, your family, and any others you can think of.

I also recommend doing a happiness spell after a deep cleanse. Once you have cleared out the old nasties you were holding on to, you will have created a void. It is always advisable to fill that void with positive energy before negative energy seeps back in.

Options

Colour	Yellow, orange, pink
Carrier Oil	Sunflower
Dressing Direction	Dress your candle towards you to draw in happiness
Herb/Oil	Basil, daisy, dragon's blood, hawthorn, lavender, lemon, marigold, marjoram, parsley, sunflower, yarrow
Symbol	Smiley face, heart, circle, sun, kiss
Rune	Uruz, Gebo, Wunjo, Jera, Sowilo, Mannaz
Ogham	Huathe/Hawthorn, Ailm/Pine
Petition	Write petition in bright, sunshiny colours Draw a smiley face over the words on your petition
Number	6, 8, 9
Lunar Phase	Waxing crescent, first quarter, waxing gibbous, full
Solar Phase	Sunrise, morning, high noon
Day of the Week	Sunday for achievements and success Friday for harmony and love Wednesday for good fortune
Planet	Venus for happiness and harmony Sun for harmony and joy

Options

Zodiac Sign	Taurus for comfort and inner peace
	Cancer for home and nurturing
	Virgo for harvesting and reaping rewards
	Libra for peace and social life
Tarot Card	The Sun, the Empress, the World, the Star, Ten of Pentacles, Ace of Cups, Four of Wands, Queen of Wands, Ten of Cups
Crystal	Agate, amethyst, celestite, citrine, green aventurine, jasper, rose quartz, sunstone, tourmaline, unakite
Element	Air

Chant Suggestion

Power of wax, fire, and flame to make me happy
Work your magic and make it snappy
Happiness energy to make me smile
Cheer and joy to make it worthwhile

Extras

There are many things that make people happy. Think about what makes *you* happy and use it as part of your spell work.

+ Cake makes me incredibly happy, so I recommend putting a cupcake or cookie in front of your candle while working your spell. Eat the cake or cookie as your spell is working! (Chocolate works too.)

+ Honey symbolises happiness. Set a small dish of it in front of your candle spell. When the spell is finished, take the honey outside and tip it onto the earth as an offering.

+ Photographs or images that make you smile can be set in front of your spell working to increase the happy energy.

+ Put on your favourite uplifting music whilst you work your magic. It will raise the energy.

Friendship

A friendship spell can be worked to bring friends closer, to maintain harmony within a group, or as a request to find more friends. When sending out a call for more friends, don't use the names of specific people; keep it open. Friendship spells can also be worked to keep a connection strong when you are apart. Working on harmony is good, but working magic to keep a friend close can sometimes be more along the lines of binding, so be careful in that situation. It is advisable to bear in mind that free will is applicable here, too, just as it is in love spells.

Options

Colour	Pink, yellow
Carrier Oil	Almond, sunflower, olive
Dressing Direction	Dress the candle towards you to bring in friendship
Herb/Oil	Benzoin, cardamom, chamomile, cocoa, cinnamon, clove, copal, coriander, cumin, daisy, dandelion, dragon's blood, frankincense, geranium, ginger, hawthorn, heather, jasmine, juniper, lavender, lemon, lemon balm, marjoram, poppy, rose, rosemary, rowan, sugar, thyme, vanilla, yarrow
Symbol	Heart, circle, smiley face, triskelion
Rune	Pertho, Mannaz, Othila
Ogham	Nuinn/Ash, Gort/Ivy
Petition	Write petition in pink ink Write petition on the back of a photograph of you and friends
Number	2, 6
Lunar Phase	First quarter, waxing gibbous, full
Solar Phase	Morning, high noon
Day of the Week	Friday for friendships and relationships

Options

Planet	Sun for friendship
	Venus for relationships and happiness
	Moon for family
Zodiac Sign	Aquarius for friendships and social life
	Libra for friendships and social life
Tarot Card	Three of Cups, Two of Cups, Knight of Cups
Crystal	Moss agate, rose quartz sodalite, tourmaline, turquoise
Element	Water, earth

Chant Suggestion

Candle energy and power that lends
Bring together my circle of friends
Love and friendship ties are bound
Happiness and harmony are found

Extras

Friendship covers many areas: keeping friends together, resolving disputes between friends, drawing new friends to you, or even friendships in the form of familial relationships. For me, the easiest way to represent friendship is in the form of a photograph.

- Place photographs of your group of friends in front of the candle, or form a circle of them around it.
- If your friends have given you gifts or trinkets, place these around the candle.
- To resolve an issue between friends, use photographs to represent them.
- Roses symbolise friendship, particularly pink or yellow ones. Have a vase of them standing on your altar.
- To bring two friends closer together (or after an argument), use two candles, one for each person, and tie them together with ribbon.

Communication

Sometimes communication breaks down and we need to attempt to resolve it. Other times, we may want to work some magic to improve clear communication before an important meeting or presentation. With that being said, communication is not always identified as speech; there are many forms of communicating with other people, perhaps in ways you hadn't even thought of. A candle magic spell can open up lines of communication in all forms.

Options

Colour	Blue, yellow
Carrier Oil	Almond, coconut, sesame
Dressing Direction	Dress the candle towards you to bring in clear speech
Herb/Oil	Cardamom, cloves, coffee, juniper, lavender, mustard
Symbol	Circle, smiley face
Rune	Ansuz
Ogham	Muinn/Bramble, Edhadh/Aspen
Petition	Write petition in blue ink Print out petition so the words are clear Write petition on a telephone bill
Number	3, 8
Lunar Phase	Waxing crescent, full
Solar Phase	Mid-afternoon
Day of the Week	Wednesday for communication
Planet	Mercury for communication The Sun for communication
Zodiac Sign	Gemini for communication
Tarot Card	Five of Swords, Two of Swords, the High Priestess, Knight of Swords, Five of Wands, Seven of Swords, Four of Cups, Page of Swords, King of Swords

Options

Crystal	Blue lace agate, celestite, fluorite, hematite, moonstone, pyrite, quartz, turquoise
Element	Air

Chant Suggestion

Power of the flame and air
Help me to communicate with flair
Articulate, concise, and clear
Guide me to speak with no fear

Extras

Nowadays, there are lots of objects that can represent communication.

+ Place your mobile phone beside your spell to symbolise communication.
+ If you need to communicate with a particular person, prop their photograph by your spell.

CHAPTER FOURTEEN

Spells to Cast Out

Before you even think about asking the Universe to send truckloads of positive energy your way, you need to make room for it. I always recommend having a good emotional, mental, and spiritual clear-out before calling in positivity. Be mindful that releasing will leave a void, and nothing loves a void more than negative energy. Once you have created space, fill it with positive energy.

This chapter has spells for releasing negative energy and spells for working through it. Stress is a big obstacle for many of us; candle magic is here to help you steamroll it away. On very rare occasions, you may feel you have been hexed; I have included a section that can help you clear that energy. Also on very rare occasions, you may feel the need to send out a curse. There is a section on cursing as well, but be mindful of what you are putting out there, and take responsibility for it.

Releasing

Holding on to negative energy or old grievances can be detrimental to your mental, emotional, and physical health. You need to let go and release those demons. Candle magic is a really good way to clear out stagnant and festering emotional baggage so you can make way for all the new, fresh, good stuff.

Options

Colour	Black, white
Carrier Oil	Coconut, sesame, almond
Dressing Direction	Dress the oil away from you, as you are releasing energy
Herb/Oil	Bay, bergamot (orange), cedar, chamomile, copal, coriander, fennel, frankincense, hawthorn, juniper, lavender, lemon, lungwort, mint, myrrh, parsley, pine, rosemary, sage, salt, star anise, thyme
Symbol	Waning crescent moon, water element triangle
Rune	Hagalaz, Berkana
Ogham	Edhadh/Aspen
Petition	Write with black ink on white paper Write on a large sage leaf
Number	4, 5, 6
Lunar Phase	Waning gibbous, third quarter, waning crescent
Solar Phase	Afternoon, sunset
Day of the Week	Saturday for banishing and cleansing Wednesday for change
Planet	Moon for transformation and to dispel negative energy Saturn to dispel negative energy
Zodiac Sign	Virgo for purification Aries for purification and renewal Scorpio for renewal
Tarot Card	Hanged Man, Death, the Devil, the Tower, Four of Swords, Six of Swords

Options

Crystal	Black obsidian, fluorite, jasper, malachite, moss agate, orange calcite, pyrite, smoky quartz, sodalite, tiger's eye, tourmaline, unakite
Element	Water

Chant Suggestion

Candle magic, flame and fire release
Dispel, purify, and allow my worries to decrease
Teach me how to just let go
Show me how to go with the flow

Extras

This sort of magic is all about letting go, taking out the trash, and getting rid of that which no longer serves—basically, having a good clear-out. Make sure you throw away every remnant of a releasing spell; you want to get rid of it all.

+ After the spell is finished, tear up your petition and flush it away.
+ After the spell is finished, crumple up your petition and burn it or throw it in the trash.
+ Water is the perfect way to symbolise cleansing and releasing. Set a bowl of water in front of your candle during your spell work. Drop your petition into the water, allowing it to dissolve as part of the spell.

Cleansing and Purifying

Candle magic can be used to cleanse and purify your body, energy field, house, or ritual space, just as you would do with smoke. Candles can also cleanse and purify your magical tools or crystals: carry a lit candle around your home, or pass items just above the flame.

Options

Colour	White, blue
Carrier Oil	Coconut
Dressing Direction	Dress the candle away from you to cleanse
Herb/Oil	Fennel, geranium, ginger, lavender, lemon, mint, parsley, rosemary, garden sage, salt, star anise, thyme
Symbol	Pentagram, moon, sun, triquetra, triskelion
Rune	Laguz, Berkana
Ogham	Beith/Birch, Ngeadal/Broom, Ur/Heather, Straif/Blackthorn, Ailm/Pine
Petition	I do not use a petition when cleansing and purifying my house/tools
Number	4, 9
Lunar Phase	Waning crescent, third quarter, waning gibbous, full
Solar Phase	Afternoon, sunset
Day of the Week	Saturday for banishing and cleansing Monday to dispel illusions
Planet	Moon to dispel negative energy Saturn to dispel negative energy Sun for renewal and transformation
Zodiac Sign	Virgo for purification Aries for purification and renewal Scorpio for renewal
Tarot Card	Hanged Man, Death, the Devil, the Tower, Four of Swords, Six of Swords
Crystal	Amber, blue lace agate, fluorite, garnet, labradorite, moonstone, moss agate, obsidian, orange calcite, quartz, rose quartz, selenite, turquoise
Element	Water, air, fire

Chant Suggestion

Candle magic, flame and fire
Cleanse and purify that which I require
Negative energy now be gone
Bring in positive energy to count on

Extras

Water and salt are both excellent for cleansing and purifying and can easily be incorporated into candle magic.

- Set a bowl of salt water in front of your candle during the spell. You can sprinkle it on yourself, your home, or your magical tools once the spell is done.
- Rinse your candle in salt water before you dress it to add another layer of energy.
- Light incense alongside your candle magic spell to boost the cleansing energy.
- Fill a small dish with laundry liquid, washing-up liquid, or soap. Set it in front of your candle spell to represent cleansing.
- Make a tiny besom out of twigs. Use it to fan the cleansing energy from your candle spell.
- Use a feather to fan the cleansing energy from your candle spell.
- Arrange a circle of feathers around your candle spell to add to the energy.

Removing Obstacles

Life has a tendency to put things in our way. There are almost always blockages to remove or obstacles to overcome. Work some candle magic to clear it all away so you are free to move forward.

Options

Colour	Black, white, red
Carrier Oil	Coconut, sunflower

Options

Dressing Direction	Dress the candle away from you to remove blockages
Herb/Oil	Bergamot (orange), chillies, geranium, ginger, heather, lungwort, mint, salt, star anise
Symbol	Cross, pentacle, arrow
Rune	Naudhiz, Hagalaz, Berkana
Ogham	Huathe/Hawthorn, Onn/Gorse
Petition	Write petition in black ink Burn petition to remove the obstacles
Number	5
Lunar Phase	Waning gibbous, third quarter
Solar Phase	Afternoon, sunset
Day of the Week	Saturday for banishing, cleansing, and clearing out
Planet	Moon to dispel negative energy Saturn to dispel negative energy Sun for energy and power
Zodiac Sign	Aries to overcome obstacles Scorpio to banish Pisces to banish
Tarot Card	Two of Cups, the Chariot, Strength
Crystal	Fluorite, hematite, lapis lazuli, obsidian, pyrite, smoky quartz, tiger's eye
Element	Fire, water

Chant Suggestion

Candle magic, powerful and strong
Remove all obstacles in my way, and do not take long
Clear the path, clear the way
Obstacles removed, I do say

Extras

This sort of spell is all about moving things that are in your way, so pick items that you feel represent that intent.

- Place some bleach or cleaning fluid beside your spell (not too close!) to symbolise removing.
- Circle your spell with erasers to represent removing.

Stress Relief

Stress has a nasty habit of creeping up on us for whatever reason. Your stress might be due to your work load, home life, health, or any number of reasons. Once you realise you are stressed, improving the situation may feel overwhelming. Start by considering the mundane ways you could relieve stress. Can you solve your problem in a practical way? In any case, magic can help you along. It can clarify the cause of your stress and give you strength to overcome it.

Options

Colour	Black, blue, pink
Carrier Oil	Coconut, sesame, sunflower
Dressing Direction	Dress the oil away from you to release the energy
Herb/Oil	Cloves, coriander, lungwort, thyme, water
Symbol	Waning crescent moon, water element triangle
Rune	Hagalaz for release Berkana for release Laguz for emotions
Ogham	Edhadh/Aspen for releasing negativity Fearn/Alder for emotions Saille/Willow for emotions
Petition	Write petition in black ink on white paper, representing the balance that is needed Write petition on paper and crumple it up rather than folding it—definitely helps with stress relief!

Options

Number	4
Lunar Phase	Third quarter, waning gibbous, full
Solar Phase	Sunset
Day of the Week	Monday for emotions
Planet	Venus for emotions Moon for emotions
Zodiac Sign	Scorpio for emotions
Tarot Card	Hanged Man, Ace of Cups, Temperance, Four of Cups
Crystal	Agate, citrine, jasper, labradorite, lapis lazuli, malachite, obsidian, rose quartz, sunstone, turquoise
Element	Water

Chant Suggestion

Power of magic, candle flame
Bring me relief with no blame
Release the stress and let it go
Bring in calm and peace; make it so

Extras

Blow off some steam by tapping into your stressful energy as you work your spell—crumple, tear, or toss as needed. Let it all out!

+ Find a way to include throwing something away in your spell work. For example, visualise a pebble absorbing your stress, then throw it in the sea.

+ Tear or screw up your petition as part of the working to relieve some stress.

+ Smash an egg as part of your spell working to help relieve stressful energy.

Uncrossing and Unhexing

Being hexed or cursed is rare. To be honest, few people have the power to work such magic. And, of course, if you believe you have been cursed, then you yourself have created a negative bubble that feeds your own self-imposed curse. In any case, if you feel the need to clear a curse, candle magic does the job.

Options

Colour	Black, grey, white
Carrier Oil	Coconut, sesame
Dressing Direction	Dress the candle away from you
Herb/Oil	Blackthorn, chillies, ginger, star anise, thorns
Symbol	Pentagram, X
Rune	Thurisaz
Ogham	Straif/Blackthorn
Petition	Write with black ink on white paper
Number	5
Lunar Phase	Dark, waning gibbous, third quarter, waning crescent
Solar Phase	Afternoon, sunset
Day of the Week	Saturday for banishing, cleansing, and protection
Planet	Mars for assertion, conflict, and defence
Zodiac Sign	Gemini for uncrossing
Tarot Card	Any of the following cards, but turn them upside down so they are in reverse: Temperance, Two of Swords, Eight of Swords, the Hanged Man
Crystal	Amethyst, bloodstone, carnelian, hematite, jasper, malachite, smoky quartz, tiger's eye
Element	Fire

Chant Suggestion

I clear and deflect this hateful curse
That it may do no more to hurt
Break the hex; it can do no worse
By this candle, the curse avert

Extras

If you are experiencing a period of bad luck, use these suggestions to clear the air.

- Use hot and spicy ingredients such as chillies and pepper—things that have heat—to burn away the curse.
- Tear or rip up your petition with force. Burn the pieces.
- Make actions that symbolise strength to break the negative energy.
- Use scissors to cut your petition.
- Place a blade in front of your candle to symbolise cutting the cords to any negative energy.
- Allow your candle to burn partway and then snuff it out. Snap the candle in half to break the curse.
- Allow your candle to burn partway, then quickly turn it upside down into a tray of sand or dirt, snuffing out the flame and stopping the curse.

Cursing

A curse is a malevolent spell cast with the intention of harm. Cursing is not something that I do on a regular basis, and it is definitely not magic that should be worked whilst you are angry. No magic should be worked when you are angry, but cursing is a particularly bad idea. Sending baneful magic out into the world while angry can be dangerous; an angry mind can make mistakes.

On occasion, you may feel the need to curse someone. Think it through carefully. Take responsibility for the magic that you put out there. Only you can decide whether sending out a curse is the right thing to do—that choice is yours alone to make.

As with all spell work, there is a state of checks and balances. Whatever you put into the world does come back at some point; you need to be aware of this. Really think about the situation and whether it can only be resolved by this action. Make sure that whatever magical action (or reaction) you make is warranted. Cursing is not for the fainthearted, and I urge you not to take it lightly. Before setting things in motion, be very, very sure the person you are targeting is the person responsible for your distress. I also suggest thinking about doing a binding instead. If you decide cursing is the right course of action, then candle magic can help.

Options

Colour	Burgundy, black
Carrier Oil	Almond, sesame
Dressing Direction	Dress the candle away from you
Herb/Oil	Chillies, dragon's blood, rowan, yarrow
Symbol	Pentagram, X
Rune	Hagalaz
Ogham	Ruis/Elder
Petition	Write with black ink on dark paper Write curse on the back of a photograph of the target
Number	1, 5
Lunar Phase	Dark
Solar Phase	Sunset
Day of the Week	Saturday for banishing, binding, and justice
Planet	Mars for aggression, assertion, and conflict
Zodiac Sign	Scorpio for banishing and personal power Pisces for banishing and action
Tarot Card	The Devil, the Tower

Options

Crystal	Agate, carnelian, jasper, obsidian, pyrite, tourmaline, turquoise
Element	Fire

Chant Suggestion

Candle magic with the power to harm
Let this curse be upon [name] and work like a charm
This curse to them I now serve
That the Universe delivers to them what they deserve

Extras

When working spells, there is always an effect. After all, you are manipulating energy. With curses in particular, you need to be aware that you are putting negative energy into the world. Take responsibility for putting a curse out there, and be mindful that it may come back to you.

+ Pin a photograph of the target to your candle with a thorn or nail.

+ Place a circle of pins, nails, or thorns around the candle.

+ Cast a circle of salt to bring in protection for yourself. I don't tend to cast a circle when working spells, but it is wise to do so when working Witch curses.

+ If you can get hold of hair, nail clippings, or something similar from your target, these can be included in the candle spell to make a personal connection.

+ Take all the spell remnants and throw them in the trash. You don't want to keep them on your property. Add extra insult by dropping all the remnants, including the petition, into a used dog poop bag before disposing.

CHAPTER FIFTEEN

～

Dedicated Candle Use

Candles are not just for spell work! They have so many other uses, particularly in Witchcraft. As such, I have included some suggestions for how to use them in ritual, and also how to work with candles dedicated for specific use. There is something very special about a candle you have dressed and dedicated to a particular deity or element. You could even dedicate a candle to your meditation practice. Try meditating with a candle you have dedicated purely for that purpose—you will really feel a difference in energy. The same goes for divination; I use a dedicated divination candle for tarot readings. It really helps create the right atmosphere and boosts my psychic connection. The options are limitless! What will you dedicate your candles for?

Candles in Ritual

Candles are probably one of the most-used tools in any kind of ritual. They can be used on the altar, to cast a circle, to represent deity, to mark the quarters/directions, to provide illumination, to cleanse and purify the sacred space, and, of course, to work spells.

I like to use candles to mark the quarters in a ritual. I tend to use a different colour for each element; my preferred choices are green for earth, yellow for air, red for fire, and blue for water. I place the candles at each compass point before I begin the ritual. As I call in the quarters, I light each candle in turn. Once my ritual is complete, I snuff out each candle as I release the quarters. These candles can be saved and used again in another ritual for the same purpose. If your ritual is outside and you have the space, large garden candles or torches are particularly useful for this purpose.

When you cast a circle, you can walk the boundary while carrying a lit candle to help visualise, although a lantern is easier and safer to use for this purpose.

A candle can be used to cleanse and purify your sacred space before you begin your ritual. I like to use a scented candle for cleansing and purifying, but you can use a plain one. I walk the circle holding a lit candle, visualising the light clearing, cleansing, and purifying the area.

Tea lights placed in clean jam/mason jars make an excellent labyrinth or spiral walk. Mark out the design on the ground and then set down tea light jars at regular intervals. Once they are all lit, this makes a wonderful sight and experience.

Candles you have created for a specific purpose (such as a deity or meditation candle) can be charged with intent and then used, or you could dedicate them within a candle ritual.

Practice

Candle Dedication Ritual

Use this ritual to dedicate a candle for any intent and purpose.

You will need

4 candles to represent the four quarters (I use green for earth, yellow for air, red for fire, and blue for water)

4 candleholders

Lighter or matches

A candle to dedicate

Decide where your circle is to be cast. Set the scene by placing the element candles in safe holders, then arranging them at each cardinal compass point (earth in the north, air in the east, fire in the south, and water in the west). Don't light them yet! Place the candle to be dedicated in the centre of where your circle will be.

Cast your circle by walking the boundary clockwise, visualising a protective circle around, above, and below. Say:

Cast this circle with energy and light
Candle magic contained within
Now let this ritual begin

Walk to the north and light your earth candle. Say:

Element of earth, I welcome you

Walk to the east and light your air candle. Say:

Element of air, I welcome you

Walk to the south and light your fire candle. Say:

Element of fire, I welcome you

Walk to the west and light your water candle. Say:

Element of water, I welcome you

Now walk to the centre of the circle so you have the candle to be dedicated in front of you.

Hold the candle up and ask that the candle be dedicated for whatever purpose you need. State the purpose of the candle out loud, and be clear about the intent. For example, if your candle is for meditation purposes, then describe what you would like your candle to be for you and what energy you need it to hold. If the candle is dedicated to a deity, say that; perhaps describe the qualities of the deity and what you would like from them.

Once you feel you are done, you can close down the ritual. Start by walking to the west and snuffing out the water candle. Say:

Element of water, I thank you for your energy

Walk to the south and snuff out the fire candle. Say:

Element of fire, I thank you for your energy

Walk to the east and snuff out the air candle. Say:

Element of air, I thank you for your energy

Walk to the north and snuff out the earth candle. Say:

Element of earth, I thank you for your energy

Now walk the boundary of the circle counterclockwise, visualising the sphere of protection you created dissipating into the air. Your dedicated candle is now ready for use.

Perhaps pour a little wine, milk, or honey outside as a thank you.

Candles for the Sabbats

If you work with the Wheel of the Year, you can create beautiful candles to add to your altar for each celebration or to use in sabbat rituals. They can be created using any type of candle. Dress and decorate with herbs, oils, and symbols that you associate with each celebration. I've included suggestions a little later on.

If you are not familiar with the Wheel of the Year, it was devised in the mid-twentieth century by Gerald Gardner, founder of modern Wicca, and Ross Nichols, founder of the Order of Bards, Ovates, and Druids (OBOD). The idea was influenced by the scholar Jacob Grimm in his work *Teutonic Mythology*, dated 1835 CE. The modern version of the Wheel of the Year includes the solstices and equinoxes along with four Celtic festivals; in total, there are eight sabbats spread throughout the year.

The Wheel of the Year provides a good structure for celebrating the changing of the seasons. Each sabbat corresponds to the agricultural events that take place at that time of year, as well as the weather. However, the Wheel of the Year was designed in Britain, so it might not align with the climate you live in. (It doesn't always align with the idiosyncrasies of British weather either!) And of course, in the Southern Hemisphere, the sabbats are opposite.

I tend to work more with what is happening in nature in my local area rather than the dates on the calendar, but the Wheel of the Year is a good starting point and does help us connect with our surroundings. By dressing your altar with seasonal or sabbat-related items, you are connecting to nature *and* to the area you live in.

Candles are an excellent way to bring that connection to your altar, or even to your living space. Whether or not you work with the sabbats, you can create a candle for each month of the year or for each season. Candles make excellent focal points for seasonal displays! When you decorate them for each sabbat/season, make sure to include items from outside, such as leaves, flowers, and seeds, depending on what is growing at the time.

In the following sections, I have provided an overview of each sabbat, as well as suggested candle magic ingredients. I have also included a generic blessing for each sabbat. Say the blessing as you decorate your candle to imbue it with energy for the celebration. The candle can then be placed on your altar or around your home. When the candle is lit, it will bring in the magic of the sabbat.

Personal Notes

I use small pillar candles for my sabbat candles; they are a nice size to for decorating, especially with different symbols.

I set my sabbat candles in decorated candleholders. As an example, for Yule, I arrange holly and ivy around the base of the candleholder, and for Lughnasadh, I add stems of corn or wheat.

Spring Equinox or Ostara

Northern Hemisphere: 20–23 March

Southern Hemisphere: 20–23 September

Pagans may refer to this sabbat as Ostara or Eostre. The spring equinox is all about fertility, fresh growth, and new beginnings. It is the time of year when we begin to see the first signs of spring—hopefully! The trees will have buds, and plant shoots will begin to appear from beneath the soil. The spring equinox is also a time of balance because the day and night are of equal length. There is a sense of excitement during this time of year, a promise of what is to come. The warmer days might even bring a few bees or butterflies to your garden.

OPTIONS

Colour	Pastel pink, green, pale yellow
Carrier Oil	Almond
Herb/Oil	Honeysuckle, jasmine, lavender, lemon balm, marjoram, oak, rose, thyme
Symbol	Eggs, a new shoot

CHANT SUGGESTION

Magic as it turns, the Wheel of the Year
I bless this candle as Ostara draws near

Beltane

Southern Hemisphere: 1 May
Northern Hemisphere: 1 November
The Beltane sabbat is a fire festival full of sassy energy. Building on the fertility energy of the spring equinox, Beltane is full of potential and "go get 'em" energy. The Celtic word *Beltane* translates as "the fire of Bel," and it most definitely is fiery. At this time of year, nature is in full bloom, the birds are nesting, and the earth is full of rising energy. Growth, passion, and fertility abound.

OPTIONS

Colour	Orange, red
Carrier Oil	Olive
Herb/Oil	Coriander, dragon's blood, frankincense, hawthorn, marigold, marjoram, nettle, rose
Symbol	Flame

CHANT SUGGESTION

Magic as it turns, the Wheel of the Year
I bless this candle as Beltane draws near

Summer Solstice or Litha

Northern Hemisphere: 20–23 June

Southern Hemisphere: 20–23 December

The summer solstice, also called Litha in the modern Pagan community, celebrates the longest day and shortest night, so this day is definitely full of solar energy. At this time of year, there should (hopefully) be some nice, warm weather, and the garden should be full of sweet-smelling flowers. Bees, butterflies, and insects will be out in droves, buzzing about. This is said to be the time when the veil between our human world and the realm of fairy is open.

The summer solstice is the halfway point of the year. (Midsummer is another name for this date in the calendar.) Nature is in the growing season, and from this point forward, we begin the harvest.

OPTIONS

Colour	Yellow, gold
Carrier Oil	Sunflower
Herb/Oil	Basil, chamomile, fennel, heather, honeysuckle, lavender, oak, parsley, pine, rosemary, rowan, sage, sunflower, thyme
Symbol	Sun

CHANT SUGGESTION

Magic as it turns, the Wheel of the Year
I bless this candle as the summer solstice draws near

Lughnasadh

Northern Hemisphere: 1 August

Southern Hemisphere: 1 February

Bring on the harvest for Lughnasadh! Harvesting does not just take place in the fields. This is the time to harvest what we have sown for ourselves and in our own lives over the previous months. Wildflowers will be in full swing out in the meadows and hedgerows at this time of the year. Celebrate all that Mother Nature provides for us in all its glorious forms.

The name *Lughnasadh* comes from the Irish sun god, Lugh. This festival is sometimes referred to by the name Lammas from the old English "loaf mass," a time when the first loaves were blessed by the church.

OPTIONS

Colour	Orange, mustard yellow
Carrier Oil	Sunflower
Herb/Oil	Basil, frankincense, heather, marigold, mint, poppy, rose, sunflower, yarrow
Symbol	Wheatsheaf

CHANT SUGGESTION

Magic as it turns, the Wheel of the Year
I bless this candle as Lughnasadh draws near

Autumn Equinox or Mabon

Northern Hemisphere: 20–23 September
Southern Hemisphere: 20–23 March
The autumn equinox, also called Mabon or Harvest Home in the modern Pagan community, celebrates the harvest but welcomes the autumn in too. This is a month of gratitude for all that was harvested as well as a month of balance, thanks to the equinox. Berries and nuts should all be ready to pick at this time of the year. The weather may still be warm and sunny, but first thing in the morning, there will be currents of fresh, crisp air. I like to take this time to have an autumn clear-out; I give everything a fresh sweep.

OPTIONS

Colour	Brown, burnt orange
Carrier Oil	Sunflower
Herb/Oil	Benzoin, chamomile, frankincense, marigold, myrrh, oak, rosemary, sage, sunflower, yarrow
Symbol	Leaf

CHANT SUGGESTION

Magic as it turns, the Wheel of the Year
I bless this candle as the autumn equinox draws near

Samhain

Northern Hemisphere: 31 October

Southern Hemisphere: 1 May

Samhain, meaning "summer's end," is the season of the Witch. It is also a time to honour our ancestors and remember those that have gone before us. This represents the last and final harvest of the season as preparations begin for the winter months. The woods and forests will be displaying their beautiful autumn colours. Nature will be full of spiders, and their webs are ready to trap unsuspecting insects or humans! Samhain shares a date with Halloween, originally a Celtic festival that is now known for trick-or-treating and lots of candy.

OPTIONS

Colour	Black, deep red
Carrier Oil	Olive
Herb/Oil	Bay, heather, nettle, oak, patchouli, pine, rosemary, sage, sunflower; if you find pumpkin spice mix in the shop at this time of year, you can roll your candle in it to bring in the energy of the season
Symbol	Pumpkin

CHANT SUGGESTION

Magic as it turns, the Wheel of the Year
I bless this candle as Samhain draws near

Winter Solstice or Yule

Northern Hemisphere: 20–23 December

Southern Hemisphere: 20–23 June

'Tis the season to be jolly! And to celebrate the winter solstice, also called Yule in the modern Pagan community. This sabbat honours the shortest day and longest night of the year as we welcome back the sun. There is an immense wave of festive energy at this time, particularly in the weeks building up to the sabbat. Focus on the important parts of this festival: family, friends, and giving to others. Nature will begin to hunker down for the cold months. Cold, dark evenings are a good time to do inner work.

OPTIONS

Colour	Dark green, red
Carrier Oil	Almond
Herb/Oil	Cedar, cinnamon, cloves, frankincense, holly, myrrh, nutmeg, oak, pine, rose
Symbol	Holly leaf

CHANT SUGGESTION

Magic as it turns, the Wheel of the Year
I bless this candle as Yule draws near

Imbolc

Northern Hemisphere: 2 February

Southern Hemisphere: 1 August

Imbolc brings the very first stirrings of spring. Beneath the soil, Mother Earth begins to awaken. Although in a lot of places the ground is still covered with snow, Mother Earth is there, just under the surface. The weather will be cold, but there will be hints—just slight ones—that new beginnings are about to occur. The word *Imbolc* means "in the belly," which could represent the time of lambing.

Imbolc is ripe with expectation and anticipation. This time is about planning and plotting, doing your homework, and setting new ideas and ventures into motion.

OPTIONS

Colour	White
Carrier Oil	Almond

OPTIONS

Herb/Oil	Basil, benzoin, chamomile, coriander, dragon's blood, frankincense, heather, myrrh, rosemary, sage, witch hazel
Symbol	Candle flame

CHANT SUGGESTION

Magic as it turns, the Wheel of the Year
I bless this candle as Imbolc draws near

Element Candles

I love using candles to represent the quarters, which are the elements in ritual. I light each one at the compass points as I call them in. You can use plain white candles, but I like to create candles dedicated to each element. The symbols I use on my element candles are the standard triangular shapes for the elements.

As you carve an elemental triangle into your candle, visualise the element in its physical form, then charge the candle with that energy. It can be used in ritual as a representation of a certain element, or it can be used in any spell to incorporate specific elemental energy into a working.

I have included suggestions for creating element candles as well as a blessing you might like to use once your candle is created. The colour you choose and the other ingredients you add will all contribute to the energy of the candle. Saying the blessing once the candle has been decorated will "seal the deal" and finalise its creation.

Earth

Call upon the earth element for stability, grounding, abundance, fertility, responsibility, and strength. As you create the candle, visualise the qualities of this element. In your mind, see physical representations of earth, and charge your candle with that energy. If you work with the elementals, you could call upon their power to infuse the candle too.

The following crystals, oils, and herbs are ruled by the element of earth.

OPTIONS

Colour	Brown, green
Carrier Oil	Sesame
Herb/Oil	Grass, honeysuckle, lungwort, patchouli
Symbol	Downward-facing triangle with a horizontal line
Crystal	Bloodstone, goldstone, green jasper, hematite, malachite, moss agate, orange calcite, pebble, rose quartz, smoky quartz, tourmaline, turquoise

CHANT SUGGESTION

Elements of power, I call upon earth
To charge this candle with magic and worth
Energy of mountains, rocks, and soil
Into this candle, my magic to toil

Air

Call upon the air element for intellect, clarity, communication, knowledge, direction, and intuition. As you create the candle, visualise the qualities of this element. In your mind, see physical representations of air, and charge your candle with that energy. If you work with the elementals, you could call upon their power to infuse the candle too.

The following crystals, oils, and herbs are ruled by the element of air.

OPTIONS

Colour	Yellow
Carrier Oil	Almond
Herb/Oil	Benzoin, bergamot (orange), dandelion, lavender, marjoram, mint, parsley, pine, sage, star anise
Symbol	Upward-facing triangle with a horizontal line
Crystal	Celestite, fluorite, green aventurine, grey jasper

CHANT SUGGESTION

Elements of power, I call upon air
To charge this candle with magic and care
Energy of clouds, the wind, and cool breeze
Into this candle, my magic with ease

Fire

Call upon the element of fire for passion, creativity, courage, protection, power, and manifesting. As you create the candle, visualise the qualities of this element. In your mind, see physical representations of fire, and charge your candle with that energy. If you work with the elementals, you could call upon their power to infuse the candle too.

The following crystals, oils, and herbs are ruled by the element of fire.

OPTIONS

Colour	Red
Carrier Oil	Olive
Herb/Oil	Basil, bay, black pepper, blackthorn, cedar, cinnamon, clove, coriander, dragon's blood, fennel, frankincense, ginger, hawthorn, holly, juniper, marigold, mustard, nettle, nutmeg, oak, pine, rosemary, rowan, sunflower, witch hazel
Symbol	Upward-facing triangle
Crystal	Amber, bloodstone, carnelian, citrine, clear quartz, garnet, goldstone, hematite, pyrite, sunstone, tiger's eye, unakite

CHANT SUGGESTION

Elements of power, I call upon fire
To charge this candle with magic and inspire
Energy of bonfires, hot coals, and flame
Into this candle, my magic will aim

Water

Call upon the element of water for purification, emotions, compassion, healing, and rebirth. As you create the candle, visualise the qualities of this element. In your mind, see physical representations of water, and charge your candle with that energy. If you work with the elementals, you could call upon their power to infuse the candle too.

The following crystals, oils, and herbs are ruled by the element of water.

OPTIONS

Colour	Blue
Carrier Oil	Coconut
Herb/Oil	Cardamom, chamomile, daisy, geranium, heather, jasmine, lemon balm, myrrh, oak, poppy, rose, thyme, yarrow
Symbol	Downward-facing triangle
Crystal	Amethyst, blue lace agate, celestite, clear quartz, fluorite, labradorite, lapis lazuli, moonstone, rose quartz, selenite, sodalite, unakite

CHANT SUGGESTION

Elements of power, I call upon water
To charge this candle with magic of the quarter
Energy of rivers, oceans, and seas
Into this candle, my magic with ease

God and Goddess Candles

In many Wiccan traditions, candles are placed on the altar to represent the God and the Goddess and/or male and female energies. Often these are pillar or taper candles, although you could use shaped figure candles. Regardless of candle type, choosing a gold candle for the God and a silver candle for the Goddess works well. I would begin by cleansing and consecrating the candles. Then they can be decorated and dressed in oils and herbs.

Here are my suggestions if you'd like to create your own God and Goddess candles.

Options (God Candle)

Colour	Gold
Carrier Oil	Olive
Herb/Oil	Black pepper, frankincense, pine
Symbol	God symbol carved into the centre of the candle

Options (Goddess Candle)

Colour	Silver
Carrier Oil	Coconut
Herb/Oil	Geranium, lemon balm, rose
Symbol	Goddess symbol carved into the centre of the candle

Deity Candles

You can dedicate a candle to a specific deity. To begin, select a candle that you associate with a certain deity, or one deity directs you to choose. Cleanse and consecrate the candle, then dress it in oils and/or herbs that are specific to that deity. This candle can be placed on your altar and lit each time you wish to connect with that deity. This section has two examples, using deities I work with. Since you will likely want to work with deities not listed here, I've included my reasonings in the Options table in the hopes that they inspire you as you choose your own spell ingredients.

The Cailleach

The Cailleach has walked beside me for many years; she is my main matron deity. The Cailleach is a Neolithic goddess with origins in ancient Britain (primarily Scotland and Ireland), but stories of her can be found across Europe and even further afield. She is a goddess of the ancestors, wisdom, and rebirth. As a winter goddess, the time when she is most powerful and present runs from October to the end of April. Stories describe her as a creation goddess, creating the landscape by dropping boulders from her apron. She is a Crone figure with blue skin and a strong character that does not tolerate any nonsense!

OPTIONS

Colour	Light blue, turquoise (the colour of her skin)
Carrier Oil	Almond (brings the magic of intuition and psychic powers, both of which the Cailleach works with)
Herb/Oil	Patchouli (a feminine, protective herb that is ruled by the earth element, to reflect the land of the Cailleach)
Symbol	Spiral (reflects the Crone aspect and the cycle of life, both of which can be found within the Cailleach)

Belenus Candle

Belenus has walked with me for a few years now. He is almost an opposite to the Cailleach, as his time is during the warmer summer months. His story began in the English county of Lancashire, though he was worshiped throughout Britain and Europe. His name translates as "bright or shining one," and he most definitely is full of solar power and all the characteristics the sun brings with it.

OPTIONS

Colour	Yellow (to represent his solar aspects)
Carrier Oil	Sunflower (masculine; ruled by the fire element and the sun; brings the magic of strength, courage, confidence, and happiness)
Herb/Oil	Cinnamon (masculine; ruled by the fire element and the sun; brings the magic of success, healing, power, protection, and psychic abilities) Orange bergamot (masculine; ruled by the sun and Mercury; brings solar energy and success) Sunflower seeds (masculine, ruled by the fire element and the sun; bring protection, truth, and happiness)
Symbol	Sun

Animal Guide Candles

Many cultures across the globe have a history of working with animal guides from the spirit world. I work with my animal guides regularly, and I like to have a particular candle on my altar dedicated to my main guide. These candles can be used to connect with your animal guide in the spirit realm, in meditation, or when you want to request that they lend their energy to your spell working. The candle can also be lit when you need to ask your guide to provide you with insight, guidance, or support.

When I need to work with a particular animal's energy in a spell, I create a small spell candle dedicated to that animal and use it for just that one spell. For my main animal guide candles, I use pillar candles that I set on my altar and light on a regular basis.

This section has two examples, using animals I work with. Since you will likely want to work with animals not listed here, I've included my reasonings in the Options table in the hopes that they inspire you as you choose your own spell ingredients.

Wild Boar Candle

My main guide is a wild boar. I have a candle that represents him and his energies on my altar.

OPTIONS

Colour	Brown (to match his fur, although I have an incredibly special boar and he loves a bright pink candle— always listen to your guides' requests)
Carrier Oil	Sesame (masculine and full of fire energy, echoing the energies of my wild boar; brings the magic of protection and strength)

Herb/Oil	Bay (masculine and full of fire energy, echoing the energies of my wild boar; brings the magic of strength, protection, and power) Cinnamon (masculine and full of fire energy, echoing the energies of my wild boar; brings the magic of psychic powers, protection, and spirituality) Cumin (masculine and full of fire energy, echoing the energies of my wild boar; brings the magic of peace, love, and protection) Ginger (masculine and full of fire energy, echoing the energies of my wild boar; brings power and protection along with a feisty kick, which my wild boar certainly has!)
Symbol	Boar tusk, or boar tooth pressed into the candle

Magpie Candle

I work with various other animals on a regular basis, such as the magpie.

OPTIONS

Colour	Black or white (like his feathers); an oily black candle would be perfect
Carrier Oil	Almond (brings intuition and psychic powers)
Herb/Oil	Cinnamon (brings the magic of psychic powers, protection, and spirituality) Rose (brings the magic of psychic powers, knowledge, mysteries, and death and rebirth)
Symbol	A feather or some glitter (magpies love shiny things)

Animal Colours

When I create an animal guide candle, I trust my intuition for which colour to use. I suggest you do the same. If you want to work with the energy of a particular animal, meditate with it first to make a connection and ask for its help. You could take this opportunity to ask what colour it would like to be represented with—it may have a preference; it may not. Be guided by your intuition and/or the intent that you want the animal to bring with it. Keep in mind that some animals lend themselves to particular colours. Here are my suggestions:

Badger: Black or white, like its fur

Bat: Black

Bear: Brown or white, depending on the type of bear

Bee: Yellow or black, to match the colours of a bee

Butterfly: You can be creative here and use a multicoloured candle or a bright one

Crow: Black or purple, because their feathers have a beautiful sheen to them

Deer: Pale brown or orange, like their coats

Dolphin: Grey or blue, to match their skin or the waters of the ocean

Eagle: Gold, to reflect the sheen of their feathers but also the strength and courage they bring

Frog: Green, like the colour of their skin

Ladybird/Ladybug: Red, to match their colour

Lion: Yellow, for the colour of their coat and also to bring in the colour magic of strength

Peacock: Purple or blue, to match their plumage

Phoenix: Red or orange, to tie in their fiery colours

Swan: White, like their feathers

Unicorn: You could use a white candle or a shimmery pastel candle

Wolf: Grey, to match its coat

Meditation Candles

Create and dedicate a candle specifically to use in meditation. It can be set on your altar or close to the space where you meditate. Light it each time you begin meditating; it can provide focus for your session.

This candle needs to embody peace, calm, and spirituality. Generally, I would suggest a pale colour for your candle to bring about a serene energy, but you may feel that a darker colour makes more sense—trust your instincts. Scent can also improve your connection to your meditation candle. The scent needs to be something you love, because you will have to be comfortable sitting with the smell whilst you meditate.

As you create your candle, charge it and the ingredients with the intent of peace, calm, and a meditative connection. Light this candle and meditate in front of it, then snuff it out until the next time you meditate.

Options

Colour	Lilac, white
Carrier Oil	Olive oil
Herb/Oil	Frankincense, honeysuckle, jasmine; choosing scents you like is important when meditating
Symbol	I would not add a symbol, but you could draw something such as a lotus flower; I would add a little glitter, just because

Personal Notes

I use a large white pillar candle set in a round wooden holder that has a large lip so I can pop crystals around the base if I want to.

Divination Candles

When I work with tarot cards or any kind of divination, I like to light a candle. I have one that I use particularly for that purpose! Mine is a large white pillar candle that has been dedicated for use in divination. Choose a colour that you think represents psychic abilities, then add oils and herbs. The candle can be lit when you are doing a reading of any type. Leave it to burn whilst you work your divination, then snuff it out. The candle can be relit the next time you do a reading.

Options

Colour	Purple, white
Carrier Oil	Almond
Herb/Oil	Cloves, coffee beans, juniper
Symbol	I would not add a symbol; instead, push a couple of blackthorn thorns into the base of the candle for extra magic

Personal Notes

I light the same candle for all kinds of divination, whether I am reading tarot, drawing oracle cards, or using a pendulum. However, you could create a different candle for each type of divination method.

CHAPTER SIXTEEN

Elevating Your Practice

Yet *more* options for working with candles outside of spell work? Yes indeed!

Scrying and candle divination are fascinating to work with and can lead to surprising insights. Some areas of candle divination can take a bit of practice to get the hang of, but it will be worth the effort. My personal favourite is pinned candle divination—so simple and straightforward, yet great at providing clarity and answering questions. For the crafters out there, making your own candles adds another dimension to your magical workings, as you imbue the candle with your own energy right from the start. I've included exercises in this chapter that will teach you how to do just that.

At the end of this chapter, I also share other ways to practice divination using lanterns or lamps.

Candle Divination

To scry basically means to use a reflective surface to see the future or gain insight. Scrying can be done using water, crystals, smoke, or flame, among other things. Obviously, in this book, we are going to focus on the candle flame.

Pyromancy (Candle Flame Scrying)

Candle flame scrying is one of the simplest ways to scry. All you need is a candle in a safe holder and something to light it with. When I scry, I generally use a plain white candle, but you could choose a colour that aligns with your question. For instance, if your query is about your love life, you might choose a red candle. If you enjoy candle flame scrying, you may want to dedicate a large pillar candle purely for this purpose; you can snuff it out and reuse it each time you scry.

I recommend dressing the candle as you would for spell work: with oil and/or herbs that align with the subject of your question. Alternatively, you could use oils and herbs that correspond to psychic abilities.

If the querent is yourself, I recommend incorporating something that is personal to you. Perhaps place a business card or a photograph under the candle.

You will need

Candle

Safe candleholder

Lighter or matches

Notepad

Pen

Corresponding herbs/oils (optional)

If you have chosen to work with herbs and oils, dress your candle.

Find a space where you will not be interrupted. Scrying works best if you are able to practice in a darkened room; this helps the flame stand out. Make sure there are no draughts or sources of breeze.

When you have chosen your space, you can cast a simple circle of protection by visualising light surrounding you, washing over and below you to form a sphere. You may also want to play some quiet music in the background. I like to light some incense, a blend that corresponds with psychic work.

Now, you are ready to scry.

Sit quietly for a moment in front of the candle and settle yourself. Take a few deep breaths in and out. Allow all worries and cares from the day to be released.

Ask your question, either aloud or in your mind. Keep your focus on it. Light the candle.

Allow the flame to burn for a few moments, then focus on the flame. Write down any thoughts that come to mind, or symbols or images you see in the flame.

When you feel you have gained all you can, snuff out the candle.

If the flame's message did not make sense initially, set aside the notes you jotted down. Leave them for a day or two, then come back to them.

How the candle flame moves during pyromancy may also provide answers to your question. Here are some simple translations, but trust your intuition.

Flame Burns Brightly: The answer to your query is a positive one.

Flame Struggles to Burn Properly: Uncertainty, perhaps in the answer to your query, but there could also be uncertainty in regard to your commitment to the subject of the question.

Flame Suddenly Flares: Something unexpected will happen.

Flames Flickers: There is a lack of dedication to the outcome.

Wax Dripping: If the wax drips to the left of the candle (as you are facing it), it can be a negative sign. If the wax drips to the right, it may be a positive sign.

Causinomancy (Blessed Burning)

Causinomancy is divination achieved by burning items in a sacred or blessed fire. This can be achieved in candle magic by using a blessed candle. (Your candle can be blessed by charging it under moonlight or dabbing it with moon or sun water.) The items usually burnt are leaves from specific plants or slips of paper.

You will need

Blessed candle in a safe holder

Lighter or matches

Slip of paper and pen *or* natural item such as a leaf, flower, or herb

Cauldron or fireproof dish

Write your query on a slip of paper. If you prefer, choose a natural item that represents your query instead. Make sure it will not produce nasty chemical smoke when you burn it.

Hold the paper or natural item in your hands and focus on your query. Charge the item with your energy.

Light the candle.

Hold the item to the candle flame so that the edge catches fire.

Carefully drop the burning item into the cauldron.

Watch the item burn. Notice the flames and the smoke and any images or symbols you can see.

How the item burns may also provide answers to your question. Here are some simple translations, but trust your intuition.

Item Burns Quickly: The outcome will be positive, and the result may come quickly.

Item Only Partly Burns: There is a blockage. You may want to rethink your plans or work out what is holding things up.

Item Smoulders, Sputters, and Goes Out Before It Is Fully Burnt: The outcome is negative.

Item Will Not Catch Alight at All: This shows a definite negative, and you may want to stop your plans.

Capnomancy (Smoke Patterns)

Capnomancy is divination by means of reading patterns in smoke. This is not very easy to do with candle magic, but sometimes you do get a candle that sends out a decent amount of smoke; in that case, do a reading. You can practice capnomancy whilst you are in the middle of spell work or set up a candle specifically for this.

To create a capnomancy candle, choose a candle specifically for divination. Dress it with a corresponding oil and herbs if you wish. Set it in a safe holder and light it. It often helps to have a light background behind the candle so you can see the smoke clearly. It also helps to note the compass positions.

Ask a question. How the smoke moves will provide answers. Here are some simple translations, but trust your intuition.

Clear, Thin Stream of Smoke Moves Steadily Upwards: This is a positive answer.

Puffs of Dark Smoke: This means a negative result.

Smoke Blows Away from You: Your goal or outcome may take some time.

Smoke Blows Towards You: Your goal or outcome will happen quickly and with a positive result.

Smoke Heading North: This is positive, but your goal may need a boost to help things along.

Smoke Heading East: You need to make some changes to get a positive result.

Smoke Heading South: This means a quick result.

Smoke Heading West: This direction carries emotion, telling you that you need some balance.

Pinned Candle Divination

This method of divination works by placing pins into a candle, asking a question, and then reading how and where the pins fall as the candle burns.

I like to use a black or white candle for this. Either of these colours creates a general divination candle that any question can be asked of. I recommend using a spell or taper candle, as they are thin enough to stick a pin through. I use plain silver pins, usually three of them. Each pin represents part of the situation; often, my pins represent the past, present, and future. To make your reading easier, you may want to choose different colours for your pins.

Depending on your query, you can alter the colour of your candle or the colour of the pins. For a question about your love life, you could use a red candle and red-headed pins. A query about your finances might correspond with a green candle and green-headed pins.

Once you've chosen your candle and pin colours, stick the pins into the candle, near the top.

Place the candle in a safe holder and set it on a flat surface. I recommend covering the surface with a cloth to protect against wax splatter.

Ask your question, then light the candle.

Watch the flame for any signs or symbols that might relate to your query.

Keep an eye on the pins. As soon as they fall, note how they did so. What order did the pins fall in? How far away from the candle did they land? How far away from each other did they land? All these things can help you interpret the reading. For example, if the pins fell close to the candle, the situation may be close to a resolution; if they fell further away, the situation may take longer to resolve. There are no set-in-stone interpretations here. Trust your intuition as you read the fallen pins.

Ceromancy (Wax Patterns)

Ceromancy is divination by reading wax patterns. The wax patterns are created by holding a lit candle over a sheet of paper or a bowl of water and allowing the wax to drip onto the surface whilst focusing on a question. The symbols and images created in the dripped wax are then read.

Test several candle types before working with ceromancy. Not all candles drip wax successfully. I prefer to use dinner/taper candles. White candles work well for a general reading, but if your question is about prosperity, you might want to use a green candle, or perhaps a red one for a love query. I also like to dress my candle for divination purposes before beginning.

If you are going to read the wax patterns using a bowl, make sure it is large enough for you to drip wax into. For best results, choose a bowl that is dark on the inside (I often use my cauldron). Fill the bowl halfway or three-quarters full with water. Leave space—do not fill it right to the top. If you are going to read the wax patterns using a piece of paper, lay the paper on a flat surface.

Light a candle and allow it to burn for a few minutes. This will get the wax melting, giving you plenty to work with.

When you are ready, ask your question. Carefully take the lit candle and hold it over the bowl or paper, tipping it so that the melted wax drips onto the surface.

Drip plenty of wax. Keep going until you get some decent-sized shapes, then snuff the candle. I like to keep the candle and continue to use it for this purpose.

Read the shapes and images. What do they mean to you? How does one shape relate to another? If you used a bowl of water, pay attention to how the shapes move in the water.

When you are finished, pick up the cooled, hardened pieces of wax. Flip them over, as they often have more images and shapes on the underside.

I could provide a list of shapes and meanings, but they would probably only be relevant to me. In ceromancy, you need to interpret what the symbols mean to *you*. A heart shape may represent love, and a butterfly might mean transformation, but it's also possible that these symbols mean something more personal to you.

If your initial reading is not clear, light another candle in a different colour, then drip that wax onto the surface, on top of the original wax shapes.

Making Your Own Candles

I highly recommend making your own candles, if you feel drawn to; it can be very rewarding. I have experimented over the years, but I must confess that it is a craft I have had varying degrees of success with. I prefer to leave candle-making to those who are more inclined—those with the patience and skill set to create beautiful candles, which I can then purchase. With that being said, I have included a brief introduction here. These are the basics. If you decide to experiment with candlemaking (and you really should), my hope is that this information has given you a solid foundation to build on.

Wick

One of the key features of a candle is the wick. If you are making your own candle, you need to know that size matters. Most craft shops will label wicks with the size of candle they can be used for. Wicks also come in several types, such as flat braided, cored, and square braided. Each size and type of wick will work best in a certain type of candle; check the labels when purchasing. Never buy a wick without a metal tab at the base.

A final tip: before creating your candle, always soak your wick in wax for a minute or two, then allow it to cool.

Wax

There are various types of wax, and each one will react differently.[14]

Beeswax

Beeswax burns slowly and often has a slightly different colour and/or scent, depending on what flowers the bees visited. Completely natural, it can be used to make solid candles or sheets of wax. Beeswax candles have a beautiful, unique, natural scent and are smokeless.

Coconut

Coconut oil can be used to make candles, but it is soft and burns quickly. It does tend to be more expensive to purchase. Generally organic and eco-friendly, coconut wax also burns slowly.

Gel

Not really a wax at all, gel wax is a combination of mineral oil and resin. It creates a transparent candle.

Palm

Palm is a natural wax, but it is soft, so it needs to be mixed with other types of wax or stearin. It comes from hydrogenated palm oil, which has created significant eco issues, so that's something to keep in mind.

Paraffin

Commonly used in candlemaking, paraffin (or mineral wax) does need to be mixed with a small percentage of stearic acid to create a usable candle. You also need to purchase paraffin wax specifically for candlemaking; a can of regular paraffin from your general store will not work. Do remember that paraffin is a by-product of the oil industry and if not utilised in other ways (such as in candles), it would be dumped. Paraffin is a good option if you want a scented candle, as it holds onto scent well.

---

14. Both https://www.osmology.co/ and https://www.thesprucecrafts.com/ have great resources if you'd like to learn more.

RAPESEED

A hardened vegetable oil, rapeseed or canola wax is used to make several types of candle. It carries and releases scent well and burns slowly. Rapeseed is sustainable and renewable.

SOY

Soy is a more recent addition to the world of candles, and it is said to be more eco-friendly than paraffin. Soy wax is, unsurprisingly, created from the soybean and is completely natural. It creates a soft wax that needs to be supported in a container. It is often mixed with other wax types such as coconut, palm, or beeswax. Soy wax is slow burning, natural, renewable, and biodegradable.

Colour

Colour is added to candles by way of aniline dyes specifically used for candlemaking. The amount to add is based on the size of candle; consult a craft store or manufacturer. If you prefer, you can experiment with natural plant and vegetable dyes instead.

Scent

Essential oils are the best way to add scent to your candle; I would not use a perfume or chemically based scent, as that goes out into the air you are going to breathe.

Tools

You are going to need a double boiler, spoons, ladles, clips to hold the wick, and buckets to cool the moulds. Oh yes, and moulds to make the candles in.

Melt and Pour

Nowadays you can buy "melt and pour" candle wax that is already mixed and sorted for you. You literally just melt it and pour it into your container or mould.

Making Rolled Candles

I do make rolled candles myself because they are super easy.

Buy sheets of wax (usually beeswax); these come in a variety of colours. Cut them to your desired size and then set them out in the sun or place them somewhere warm until the sheet is pliable. Cut a wick to size. (You do not need a metal base tab for these.) Lay the wick on the edge of one side and roll the sheet up.

This type of candle allows you to add dried herbs and spices or drops of essential oil to the inside of the candle. You could also add tiny crystal chips! Simply sprinkle the ingredients across the sheet before you roll it up.

Making Oil Candles

Oil candles are quite easy to make and utilise old perfume or vinegar bottles.

Practice

Oil Candle, Option 1

Note: Never use mineral oil, alcohol, propane, turpentine, or pure gasoline for your oil candle or oil lamps—these can release toxic vapours.

You will need

Empty bottle or jar, washed and cleaned with any labels removed

Nylon wick

Bottle stopper

Lamp oil (special oil used specifically for lamps, made from refined kerosene or paraffin); it is possible to replace this with olive oil or castor oil

Funnel

Pour the oil into your bottle using the funnel. Pour until the bottle is about three quarters of the way full.

Put the wick into the bottle. The wick should be long enough to touch the bottom of the bottle.

Fit the bottle stopper, feeding the top of the wick up through it. Allow the wick to soak for ten minutes before lighting it.

Practice
⟳

Oil Candle, Option 2

This can also be done with easily available items.

You will need

    Empty bottle or jar

    Aluminium foil

    Cotton wool ball

    Vegetable or olive oil

Start by carefully unrolling the cotton wool ball, then cut it in half lengthways. Take the strips and twist them together; you want them fairly tight, but with enough space for air to circulate. This will be your wick.

Take a long strip of aluminium foil. Fold it over several times so that it is fairly strong. You need the finished strip to be wide enough to form a bridge across the opening of the bottle or jar, with space left on either side. Poke or cut a hole in the centre of the foil; this is what the wick will go through.

Push the wick through the hole in the foil so that there is a small amount showing, enough for you to light.

Take the foil with the wick attached and lay it across the top of your jar, dropping the long part of the wick inside the jar. Fold the ends of the foil inside the jar.

Now pour your oil into the jar; I like to fill it about three-quarters full. Allow the oil to soak up through the wick.

Add any ingredients that you want to work your spell with to the oil in the jar, then light the wick. Bear in mind that cotton wool can be a bit smoky to burn.

Practice

Oil Candle, Option 3

Here is an even simpler way to create your own oil candle.

You will need

    Clean mason/jam jar made of glass

    Water

    Floating wick (small metal disc and waxed wick)

    Vegetable oil (olive, sunflower, etc.)

    Natural items such as flowers, leaves, shells, pebbles, etc.

Fill your empty jar with natural items of your choice. Pine cones, shells, pebbles, and berries all work well, but flowers or leaves can be used too. These are for decoration and magical intent; they will not be burnt.

Fill the jar with water until all the natural items have been covered. Leave a small gap at the top of the jar.

Slowly and carefully, pour vegetable oil on top of the water; you need about 0.7 centimetres (¼ inch) of oil.

Pop your floating wick on top of the oil layer, then light it.

Note: A tablespoon of vegetable oil burns for about two hours.

Lantern and Lamp Magic

If you love candle magic, then do give lantern or lamp magic a try! Both are really interesting to work with, and can be used very successfully to work magic.

Lanterns

Lanterns offer a different type of candle magic in that the flame is shielded from the weather, so they are good for use outdoors. I cannot tell you how many times I have struggled to light candles at outdoor rituals. Lanterns are the way to go! Whether they are metal or glass, I recommend choosing a lantern with a ring on top, so you can hang or hold it, or a glass storm lantern. But you can work your candle magic with any kind of lantern, really.

If you work with tarot, you will be familiar with the Hermit. In most images, he is carrying a lantern. This symbolises the light shining in the dark; his lantern illuminates the way forward and reminds you there is hope.

One bonus of using lanterns is that they provide a neat container into which you can drop petitions and dried herbs. You can also draw sigils and symbols on the outside of the glass. Here are some other ways I'd recommend working with a lantern:

- Use your lantern for scrying. Sit in a dark room with a mirror in front of you and a lantern behind you so that the reflection of the flame is just visible in the mirror. Watch the reflection and read any symbols or signs.
- Place a lantern on your altar to remove a toxic person from your life, to dispel negative energy, or to rid yourself of bad habits. Write the name, energy, or habit on a slip of paper and pop it inside the lantern. Light the flame and leave the lantern burning on your altar until you feel it has done the work.
- Cleanse and purify your home with a lantern. Light the flame and carry the lantern throughout your home. Walk into each room and shine the light into every corner and cupboard.
- A lantern can be placed in the front window of your home to welcome your ancestors.

Lamps

Lamps offer a whole other avenue of magical workings; their flame burns hotter and often faster than a candle. You need oil for a lamp, and that serves as a carrier for essential oils and dried herbs. You can also add petitions, charms, crystals, bones, and other items into the oil container of a lamp. (Petitions can also be pinned to the wick of an oil lamp; with an oil lamp, you can also adjust the flame.) Colour can even be added to the oil for another layer of power! In this type of magical working, the oil becomes infused with the herbs and other items you add and draws that energy up through the wick as it burns.

Start by cleansing and consecrating your lamp. Wipe it with moon or spring water, or cleanse it with incense smoke. Then anoint the lamp with an essential oil blend.

All sorts of ingredients can be added to the oil in the base of the lamp. You may choose to add herbs, roots, petition papers, photographs, coins, or charms. Charge each item with your intent as you add it to the oil.

When you are ready to work your spell, light the wick.

Spend some time visualising your goal or desire.

Say a chant or speak words from the heart to direct the spell. Verbally telling the lamp what you require works well.

You can leave the lamp to burn out fully, but that can take some time. Otherwise, snuff the flame once you feel the magic has worked.

Clean the lamp inside and out before you use it again.

CONCLUSION

As the Candlelight Flickers...

I hope the information in this book has been useful! Candle magic is such an amazing area of the Craft. Although I provided correspondences and ways to add layers to your spell work, ultimately, the choice is yours. Don't take my correspondences as set in stone; if you feel something else will work instead, trust your intuition. Your intuition will never let you down.

Remember that you do not need to spend lots of money on exotic ingredients from the other side of the globe. Herbs and plants from your own garden or local market have more personal power.

You also do not need to buy fancy candles. Work with what you have—and with what fits your budget. You could keep things super simple and cast a spell with just a small white candle and nothing else. It is lighting the flame that sets the magic in motion.

Further Reading

Buckland, Ray. *Advanced Candle Magick: More Spells and Rituals for Every Purpose*. St. Paul, MN: Llewellyn Publications, 2002.

Holmes, Kylie. *Pagan Portals: Runes*. Winchester, UK: Moon Books, 2013.

Moura, Ann. *Grimoire for the Green Witch: A Complete Book of Shadows*. St. Paul, MN: Llewellyn Publications, 2003.

Norman, Ceri. *A Beginner's Guide to Ogham Divination*. Winchester, UK: Moon Books, 2022.

S, Taren. *Hoodoo in the Psalms: God's Magick*. Winchester, UK: Moon Books, 2019.

Sentier, Elen. *Numerology: Dancing the Spirals of Time*. Winchester, UK: Moon Books, 2019.

To Write to the Author

If you wish to contact the author or would like more information about this book, please write to the author in care of Llewellyn Worldwide Ltd. and we will forward your request. Both the author and the publisher appreciate hearing from you and learning of your enjoyment of this book and how it has helped you. Llewellyn Worldwide Ltd. cannot guarantee that every letter written to the author can be answered, but all will be forwarded. Please write to:

Rachel Patterson
℅ Llewellyn Worldwide
2143 Wooddale Drive
Woodbury, MN 55125-2989
Please enclose a self-addressed stamped envelope for reply,
or $1.00 to cover costs. If outside the U.S.A., enclose
an international postal reply coupon.

Many of Llewellyn's authors have websites with additional information and resources. For more information, please visit our website at http://www.llewellyn.com.